D1104819

DISCARDED

15223460

MN

PS
591
M6
B5.6
1986
c.5

BLOSSOMS & BLIZZARDS

AN ANTHOLOGY

DISCARDED

edited by:

C.J. Fosdick

Linda Essig

Laurel Winter

FE27 '92

Pegasus Prose

Rochester, Minnesota

1986

Laurel Winter

BLOSSOMS & BLIZZARDS is made
possible in part by a grant
from the Southeastern Minnesota Arts Council,
for which Pegasus Prose is grateful.

Copyright © 1986 by Pegasus Prose
All rights reserved.

First Published in simultaneous
hardcover and paperback editions by
Pegasus Prose
6423 13th Ave. NW
Rochester, MN 55901

Printed in the United States of America
by Davies Printing Company, Rochester, MN

Hardcover by Midwest Editions, Minneapolis, MN

Photographs by Gary Koenig, Rochester, MN

Cover Design by Pat Boyd, Ads & Art

ISBN 0-9617240-3-X
ISBN 0-9617240-1-3 pbk.

FOREWORD

Like many good ideas, this book started with a seed of inspiration blown in by a long, cold winter. As Carol Bly points out in her essay, "Great Snows," Minnesotans have a secret affection for bad weather. However, the six-month winter of '85-86 put a definite strain on that affection. It resurrected bumper stickers and slogans like "Forty below keeps out the riffraff," or "Minnesota — home of blonde hair and blue ears." And the all-time favorite, "Land of two seasons: Winter is coming, winter is here."

As Minnesotans, we were at a crucial threshold. Did we whine about our frozen feet or join the stoic legions who ski, shovel or chase a hockey puck around the ice? We decided to accentuate the positive and challenge the myths. Minnesota *does* have four seasons. A seasonal anthology could prove that to the world. (A book would also satisfy that egotistic desire basic to all writers — to see more of their work in print.)

Like good Minnesota farmers, we planted in spring, obtaining a seed money grant from the Southeastern Minnesota Arts Council.

Blossoms & Blizzards is the fall harvest, a collection of short stories, poems, and essays by Minnesota authors. It's a provocative mix of work by well-known Minnesota writers and some who are famous in smaller circles. Besides living and working in Minnesota, all have at least two things in common: talent and an affectionate pride in our state. That pride shines through in every selection, giving the reader a composite sketch of the Minnesota personality in a theater of seasons.

Minnesotans live longer, work harder, and dwell on quality of life. We are stoic and immodest in adversity. As Patricia Hampl puts it, "Our cold is our pride, our supremacy." She adds in the excerpt from *A Romantic Education* that "more than anything, winter made me want to write."

We are equally stoic in the heat, as Garrison Keillor relates in the witty excerpt from *Lake Wobegon Days*. And self-effacing in our pain . . . a message Jeanette Hinds delivers in her extraordinary poem, "Bachelor Uncle."

Coming to terms with our weather, making the most of what we have, is probably rooted in the variety of ethnic cultures found in Minnesota. Meridel LeSueur gloried in all the rituals and the great richness of growing up in a northwest village. "There is no place in the world with summer's end, fall harvest, and Indian summer as in Minnesota," she says in the excerpt from "The Ancient People and the Newly Come." To her, fall was like preparing for battle, with time off for celebration.

Minnesotans enjoy preparing for battle and when the weather is compliant, the battle often rages on other fronts. The current plight of the Minnesota farmer will leave its mark in Minnesota literature. John Solensten's "The Heron Dancer" is a poignant story about a Norwegian farmer fighting a system that ravages the natural order of life. Myron Bietz's "From the Frozen North" is a funny/frightening glimpse of what will be left of Minnesota 2000 years from now.

At the start of this project, the three of us were certain we would be inundated by submissions for the winter or autumn categories. There have been many surprises, not the least of which was a glut of spring and summer selections. Proof perhaps that the shorter the season, the more indelible the impression? Or perhaps it reiterates what we like best about the Minnesota mystique — that dauntless, droll humor and optimism that weathers well in extremes. Capitalizing on that optimism, we've compiled a variety of Minnesota literature to appeal to all tastes. The gopher state isn't closed for glacial repairs — yet.

C.J. Fosdick, Linda Essig, Laurel Winter
August, 1986

SPRING

C.J. Fosdick

HALLEY'S TONIC

It was the *strangest* funeral Lake City had ever seen.

Outside the blue stucco house, children bundled in snowsuits and polar boots scudded on their layered bottoms down the hill and into the driveway between two thirty-foot spruce trees. Squealing with delight, they scampered up the hill to repeat their descent. Half of Lake City was filing through the house on the hill, spilling onto the columned porch and brick veranda with their styrofoam cups of steaming cider, smiling, laughing, toasting their good health and the first day of spring.

Inside, everyone was anxious to get a glimpse of the wooden tole-painted casket in the parlor. If anyone was disappointed to find it already closed, nobody let on. Nobody needed to see the wrinkled face of an old woman to remember Halley Edberg. She was there . . . in the scent of potted herbs that cluttered every windowsill, in the bright abstract paintings that covered every wall, and in the tiny orange and blue parlor still draped with Christmas evergreen. But most of all, Halley was there dominating the room as she always did — from the flashing blue eyes and mischievous smile of the nude in the portrait that hung over the fireplace.

Aside from the blue casket with its scrolled rim of painted flowers, the portrait drew the most attention. "Is that really supposed to be Halley?" Karen Richards, the mayor's wife asked.

Without taking his eyes off the reclining nude, his honor leaned over and mumbled into his wife's ear, "Halley — fifty years ago. Heard it was painted by some artist from Little Falls, someone who knew Charles Lindbergh."

Marta Olson squeezed Karen Richard's arm and hissed into her other ear. "His name was Donovan — her lover." For a moment, Marta hesitated, then bobbing her head for emphasis, she raised her voice to accommodate more listeners. "Halley told me herself about how they used to romp *naked* in the woods, picking wild blueberries and swimming in some creek like two satyrs."

"Satyrs are masculine, I believe," the mayor laughed. "Halley might have been strange, but she was never masculine."

"I heard her hat and shoe collection was given to the County Historical Society, and most of her paintings will go to the boys' home in Red Wing," Karen said. "Maxine Larson got her fox fur."

"Good Lord, imagine how that must set in those crows' craws." Marta's head bobbed in the direction of the two old women, dressed in black and seated at the foot of the casket. Looking more abstract in the colorful room than the portrait, one nodded curtly when someone expressed sympathy; the other stole furtive glances at the portrait, then picked at imaginary pieces of lint on her black crepe skirt.

"I didn't know Halley *had* any living relatives," Karen said.

"There was bad blood between them," Marta whispered. "Halley never told me the whole story, but I knew she ran away from home when she was just a girl and she's been running from family ever since."

"They're her sisters," somebody hissed. "Here to administer the estate."

"They seem embarassed by the estate," Jack Osbourne, the choir director at First Lutheran Church said, grinning up at the young, voluptuous nude with the snapping eyes and a smile somewhere between Mick Jagger's and the Mona Lisa's.

"It's hard to imagine Halley in the same family tree with those crows," the mayor said.

Osbourne chuckled. "According to them, Halley was the nut in the tree. They've been trying to have her committed for years. Last month they sent a psychiatrist down from Minneapolis to examine her. She threw him out."

"Halley committed?" The mayor shook his head. "That makes as much sense as re-channeling the Mississippi. They must be after the estate, now that Halley's gained some professional recognition with her paintings.

"For what it's worth, I heard the crows get only the house and all this broken-down furniture," Karen pointed out.

Osbourne laughed again. "Just desserts. You'd have to be out of your mind to live with this decor." Marta's sister, Vivian, who set up the furniture displays at Peterson's Furniture and Hardware store, added that only an artist could create such an a mish-mash. Ozzie Lindquist reminded Vivian that all artists express themselves rather, uh, unconventionally.

"Ya, and Halley was a Swede," Ed Anderson interjected. "You know how unconventional dey are."

"But she was born in Minnesota," Vivian cried.

"So were most of us," Ozzie said, gesturing with his cup of cider until it splashed on Vivian's new suede boots. "Are you saying Minnesota Swedes are more inhibited?"

The debate that followed was interrupted by Maxine Larson, who approached the group with a thermal pot of freshly brewed cider and a plate of spritz cookies. "Couldn't help overhearing," she said. "Swede or not, Halley was born different. Came in with the comet, you know. Named for it, too. She always declared she was destined, like Mark Twain, to come in and go out with the comet. People who did that were eventually recognized as high muck-a-mucks, she told me."

Maxine's husband, John, held his cup out for a refill. "Sounds like a lodge title — high muck a muck! Knowing Halley, it's more likely she was poking fun of her position on this hill every spring."

"Not many people can say their funeral was this well attended," Ozzie observed.

"Ya, no one who lived to tell about it," Ed laughed.

"To Halley then," Ozzie said, offering a toast to the nude. "We'll miss the old girl."

"Miss her tonic, you mean," Vivian snapped.

For a moment, the group collectively studied their shoes.

"To hell with Halley," a voice chortled sharply.

The room fell silent. "To hell with Halley," the voice persisted. A thin red headed boy tried to hush the orange and blue parrot that sat on his shoulder — Halley's parrot, Socrates.

A few people began to titter, then whisper among themselves. The crows went into a private huddle, watching the boy squirm under the attention. Maxine rolled her eyes. "The bird probably learned that from him," she said, nodding toward the boy. "I knew it was a mistake when Halley took him in."

"Imagine!" Vivian added, "The little thief knocks her down and steals her purse, and she takes him in. He could have robbed the house clean . . . or murdered her while she slept."

"He paid for his crimes," Ed said. "Halley must have whacked some sense in him, the way he shaped up in her custody. He's even back in school now, getting top grades I hear."

"I heard that he has no family," Ozzie said. "When he left the boys' home in Red Wing, he hitch-hiked south and talked himself into some odd jobs at the old nunnery in Frontenac. Was fired when he was caught stealing from the nuns."

"Is that when he started preying on helpless little old ladies?"

"I wouldn't call Halley *helpless*." Ozzie grinned.

"To Halley, then," John said, squeaking his styrofoam cup against Ozzie's. They clicked their heels together and turned in unison to boldly salute the nude.

Maxine refilled the empty cups in the parlor and hurried back to the kitchen for another pitcher of hot cider. "This sure hits the spot," Jack Osborne called after her. "Do we get thirds?"

Strange, Maxine thought. How grief drys the mouth and fills the stomach. The cookies were hardly touched. She poured more cider from the stoneware jugs on the table into the canning kettle on the stove, then added another orange studded with cloves, just as Halley had instructed her last week. Tuesday, was it? The last time Maxine had seen her friend alive. Halley looked so pale, draped over her turquoise sofa, and it was downright morbid to see how cheerful she was about it all. Uncharacteristic, too, to see her so organized. No formal church funeral — just a closed casket at an old-fashioned wake — with plenty of hot cider and cookies Halley had baked ahead for the occasion. No doctors, no hospitals, no undertakers. "I'll go in my sleep — burn out like the tail of the comet," she'd predicted. And she was right.

Maxine was impressed by the way the boy took charge when he found Halley dead. Before she and a few other neighbors arrived to see what could be done, he had already secured the death certificate, made burial arrangements, and had Halley laid out in the casket she had designed herself. But it was Halley's will that generated more discussion in Lake City than the new marina development that fizzled a few years back. Personally, Maxine couldn't bring herself to think about writing a will. Halley not only left one — doodled with caricatures of all the principals — but posted copies in the marina, at the Kluge Insurance office, even at the Hot Fish Shop in Winona.

"To avoid any disputes," Halley had explained. Maxine wanted to protest the clause in the will that gave the boy Halley's blue Mustang and the silver tea set that had been a gift to her grandmother from the King of Sweden. The boy would surely pawn the tea set and run the car to ruin. In Maxine's mind, giving the boy the foul-mouthed parrot was more than enough. They deserve each other, she thought wryly — birds of a feather.

The last cider crock was drained long after the street lights came on and a bone-chilling night wind blew down the Wisconsin bluffs and across Lake Pepin to the Minnesota shore. Halley's relatives had decided to spend the night at the Anderson Hotel in Wabasha, where the antique decor was more conventional. From the porch, Maxine had given them directions to the landmark hotel, finally telling them to follow the steel girded cutters that were making their annual pass down the frozen river to Wabasha. After the last snowstorm, fragile new ice chewed at the boats and tinkled in the dark like broken glass.

Maxine removed and folded her apron when the last crock was rinsed and tipped to dry on the kitchen counter. Feeling drained herself, she opened a bottle of tonic left in the pantry. Drinking straight from the re-cycled pop bottle, she went through the house for the last time, checking to see that all the sticky paper cups had been picked up, and all the lights turned out.

She was going to miss her old neighbor. Like the comet she was named for, Halley was a bright light in the city known as the birthplace of water skiing. With her art classes, you always got a bottle of tonic, a lesson in horticulture, or a sample of the old lady's whimsical wit.

The parrot was inconspicuous, sleeping on the blue casket with his head tucked under a wing. On the sofa, the boy was sleeping with his arms folded tightly across his chest. She covered him lightly with an afghan and restrained herself from brushing a wisp of hair from his eyes. What would become of him? Would he be sent back to the boys home? He wasn't old enough at sixteen to make it on his own.

She pulled a long swig from the bottle and toasted the portrait before she turned out the last light. "Goodbye Halley," she whispered. Tomorrow morning the relatives would come to take the casket to the cemetery, and what was left of Halley's things would be packed up and shipped to Minneapolis.

Emil Frick of Frick and Friends, the only realtor in town who could sell old houses, was already commissioned by the relatives. In two weeks, the blue stucco house would be a tasteful beige, inside and out, with a new earth-toned carpet for the parlor and a pheasant print from the Wild Wings Gallery hanging above the fireplace. Outside, a "Friendly Frick" for sale sign would stab what was left of the crusty snowbank children once played on.

No sooner did the front door close behind Maxine when the tapping began. Weak at first, then strong as the peck of a bird's bill against wood. "To hell with Halley," the parrot chimed. "To hell with Halley."

Without moving, the boy opened his eyes and adjusted to the dark before he groped under the sofa for the hidden flashlight. He snapped on the light and focused it on the parrot. "To hell with *you*," he said. The bird fluttered to his shoulder when the boy thumped twice on the casket, then unbolted the latch and opened the lid.

He smiled down at the tiny figure of the woman in the box. Her white hair was pinned beneath the crushed bill of an orange and blue Sunkist cap, and the white letters on the navy T-shirt she wore glowed in the dim light. "I'm not getting older, I'm getting better," the shirt announced. Her white athletic shorts matched the white satin that lined the casket and the orange polished toenails on her bare feet punctuated the dark. Her skin had the pallor of a long Minnesota winter, and the blue veins in her folded hands stood out like highways on a road map. When he flashed the light on her powdered face, he could see that her smile was fixed. "Halley? Halley!"

She opened one blue eye and winked. "Almost had you for a second," she laughed. "Help me out of this contraption. I haven't been smothered in this much satin since I was baptised 76 years ago!"

The boy helped her out of the box and over to the sofa. With his hands, he kneaded her arms and legs to get the blood circulating. "You scared me good. I thought maybe the sedative was too strong, or there wasn't enough air."

"It was hot in there all right, a close second to the hot air circulating in this parlor today. Hard to sleep through juicy gossip and fake laments. Good Lord, what a bunch of hypocrites."

"There were a few highlights," the boy smiled. "Ozzie Lindquist and Ed Anderson slid down the snowbank when they left and landed under one of your spruce trees. The Olson sisters called the sheriff to haul the men home. When a squad car arrived, all of them were singing the Lutefisk Lament with Jack Osborne running around the tree, trying to direct."

"The Lutefisk Lament — how appropriate!" In an off-key soprano, Halley sang the Minnesota version of O Tannenbaum. *"O Lutefisk, O Lutefisk, — how fragrant your aroma . . . O Lutefisk, O Lutefisk, you put me in a coma . . ."* She clapped her hands. "I could hear how things perked up with the third round of cider."

"I helped things along," the boy admitted. "Almost cleaned out the pantry — pouring tonic into each new batch of cider when Maxine wasn't looking."

"You devil!" Halley's eyes brightened. "Get the silver set. Let's have one last toast before we hit the road."

"You'd better get dressed, it's supposed to drop below freezing tonight, and we've got a long drive ahead."

"I almost wish I hadn't given Maxine the fox fur."

The boy handed her the flashlight and disappeared in the dark for a minute. When he came back, he had two shopping bags. One contained boots, wool socks, sweater and slacks, the other, her old fox fur coat. "Maxine must have forgotten to take this," he winked, "in all the excitement."

She reached up to ruffle his hair. "What a smart operator you are!"

"You're my inspiration, Halley." The boy gave her a quick smile. "Now that I've found me a grandma, I'm gonna make sure she won't do anything foolish."

"Chris Johnson! Foolish is what I do best."

"I mean like repeating this performance — in a casket without air holes."

"Honey, I got 24 good years left. I'm gonna live to be a 100 and know that my friends — not a couple of crows — will be sitting at the end of the real box of bones that gets buried."

She gave him one of her famous smiles and an affectionate jab in the chest before she began pulling winter clothes over her "Florida" outfit. The rest of the things she would need were already in the car, including the strongbox with the stocks and bonds she had saved over the years. Along with a few good pieces of jewelry and the silver tea set, it was enough to get by on — maybe even enough for Chris to go to college someday.

While she poured some tonic into the demitasse cups of the silver tea set, the boy took down the nude portrait. "We can't leave this behind," he said.

"Certainly not — a Donovan original may be worth a Picasso someday."

"I would never sell this."

"I hope we don't have to. I just want to retire in comfort and spend the rest of my life surrounded by blossoms instead of blizzards . . . or crows." She paused, tracing a fingertip around the silver demitasse cup in her hand. In the dim light, she stared at him, but he knew she was seeing someone else, reviewing an old scenario from a painful past. He knew her well enough to know when something troubled her, and he knew better than to probe. There was an unspoken agreement between them — about digging into the past. It was one of the things that he liked best about the old lady. No questions, no recriminations. She accepted people on their terms, and even managed to pull a little fun out of them.

"Hey, Grandma," he said, lifting his silver cup. "We got a future now. Here's to sand castles and sunshine." Clinking the silver cups together, they laughed as the the warm tonic trickled down their throats and the parrot ran sideways across the top of the tole-painted casket.

"To hell with Halley," Socrates chirped.

"When did he learn to say that?"

"When he got tipsy one day drinking from my cup of tonic, and I cut off his supply — cold turkey."

The boy laughed. "You wouldn't do that to me, would you?"

"A boy your age doesn't need tonic — unless it's a special occasion."

"This is an occasion . . . a resurrection, you might say."

Halley's eyes twinkled with the old familiar spark. "The best kind." She sniffled against the raglan sleeve of her sweater. "God, I hate melancholy — especially at a funeral. But you know, these Minnesota cocktails just won't taste the same in Florida. Never failed to chase the cold and preserve the health."

"The whole city's going to miss your tonic, Halley."

"This recipe earned me a living, my boy." She grinned impishly. "Did you dismantle the still?"

"Saved all I could. The rest is wired for midnight."

"Just a small explosion, right?"

"Just a faulty old furnace."

The blue Mustang was on the highway when they heard the explosion, and for a moment, there was a bright flare of light in the sky over Lake Pepin. Some say it was just a shooting star. The Lake City Graphic capitalized on the coincidence when the blue house on the hill burned to rubble. It was a personal phenomenon, the paper reported. Halley's grand exit.

C.J. Fosdick was born in Milwaukee, Wisconsin, but she considers herself 99% Minnesotan. Surrounded by oak trees and a menagerie of animals, she lives with her family on a hilltop hobby farm in Rochester, Minnesota. She's been hooked on writing since age 10 when she won her first contest. She now freelances fiction and non-fiction for newspapers, local and regional magazines, and nationals like *Seventeen* and *Writer's Digest*. As a member of the Pegasus Prose editing team, she recalls the inspired advice of an old journalism teacher: "The art of writing is in knowing what to leave in the inkpot."

Linda Brown Kolter

SAILING THE BREEZES

The sky rubs your skin
As you go
Cloud catching life
With the one you love.

Two kites in full sail,
Flying high and dipping low
On the windy streams
Of understanding.

Doing cartwheels,
Your fragile form
Wheeling, rolling
In your gusty soul.

Multicolored rags braid into your tail,
A lifelong rudder growing with the years,
With struts taut and string tight,
Catching the clouds, sailing the breezes together.

Copyright © 1985 Linda Brown Kolter. Reprinted from *The Extra* by permission of the author.

Linda Brown Kolter has written all her life, even during her ten-year career as an intensive care nurse, but she didn't attempt to publish until 1985. Since moving to Rochester, Minnesota, her poems and articles have appeared in *The Extra* and in the international entertainment journal, *Performance.* She loves poetry because it is the art of saying the most, with the fewest of words.

Stanley Kusunoki

PARK POINT IN MARCH . . .

and the mottled ice reveals
the infinite subtleties of blues and greens
liquid water color washes
with equally elusive tones of earth and sky
I wander the shoreline
the scrub aspen and dune grass majestic
in their nakedness
The arching curves catch sunlight
yellow straw
pale topaz gleam in silhouette against the snow sand
the crystalline beach
I walk, my steps crunch along intruding
upon the lulling wind
the speech of ice floes and gull cries
A foreign sound
a foreign presence, I try to blend
become sand
Impossible
Too many reminders of my kind
broken bottles
wrappers, old shoes
jetsom of the shorebound who claim this strip
as their land
forgetting it is not theirs but the lake's

The big water owns
and changes its own borders, shifting, sculpting
Those who take from it
find it will take back its territory
in a rage of temper
crashing, violent
So I muse — the lake and I eyeing each other
no question of superiority
I bow to the green-gray, mottled blue
giant in repose
and turn back to the dunes and the houses beyond them
and walking, disappear
into the landlocked world
leaving no mark that the lake will remember

Stanley Kusunoki, a graduate of the University of Minnesota in Journalism, has had articles, cartoons and poetry published in *Rochester Magazine, Medical Meetings,* the *Post-Bulletin,* and the short-lived *TGIF.* As part of the 1985 Rochester Peace Rally, he read two of his poems: one about the internment of his grandfather in WW II, the other a plea and warning from the shadowgraph in Hiroshima. He lives in Rochester on the banks of the Zumbro River where he is known to fish for members of the Pulitzer Committee.

Paul Gruchow

from
JOURNAL OF A PRAIRIE YEAR

There seems in late spring to be an openness, a frankness, a guilelessness that is missing at other times of the year. I do not suppose that there is more to this than an impression. Life is never innocent.

But there is in spring the openness of the landscape itself. The trees, although green, are not yet in full leaf. One can still see sky through the canopy of a tree. In the grasslands, the vegetation has begun to green, the earliest of the flowers are in bloom, the insects are about, the spiders are at their webs, the music of the birds is in the air. Everywhere there is the motion of life as it has not been evident for months. But the grasses are just sprouting, and even the fastest growing of the forbs is yet a diminutive thing. The dense thicket of prairie growth has not yet been formed in late spring. One can still see through the shoots of things to the surprisingly bare prairie floor.

Young birds are in the shell or on the nest or they are fledgling. Despite the cleverness with which they have been domiciled, the persistent wanderer cannot help but stumble upon them. The same is true for the young of the mammals. It takes time and attention to catch a fox in action at any other time of the year, but in spring, even a modestly observant dilettante can find the occupied den of one and stake it out. There is too much youthfulness about life in the spring to keep it long hidden.

So it was that while wandering along a prairie lane one late spring evening, I came to spend a quarter of an hour in the company of a badger. I was minding my own business. I was tired and on my own time. I was not about to get into communion with anything. I simply wanted quiet and the relaxation of being aimlessly in motion.

I had gone a mile or a little more. I was beyond sight and sound of the prairie village in which I lived. The night was springishly free from pollen and insect pests. I was caught up in the absence of my own thoughts. The fact of a world beyond the extremities of my own body had entirely escaped me.

And then it aroused me — as if it were a bar of music to which I was awakening — a loud rustling in the grass at my side. It frightened me. It was such a strange, disembodied, improbably loud rustling. I stood at roadside listening for the noise in the grass again, mildly annoyed to have been interrupted so.

The rustling came again, the same loud, strange, ominous sound. It came from the bottom of the road ditch not more than ten feet away. A ripple of young grass ran up to the edge of the gravel road like a wave of water released somehow from the bondage of gravity.

From it emerged in a moment a young badger. The badger has a reputation for meanness. When it is confronted by a human, it will sometimes bare its big carnassials and begin to hiss and snarl in a most convincing manner, and it will lunge at the intruder as if to kill. A badger is not a tiny creature — an adult weighs about twenty-five pounds — and it comes low-slung, broad-skulled, pug-nosed. It is as muscled as a boxer, and it is decorated with a white racing stripe down the center of its head. It looks like a fat little bomb.

Those who have stood their ground (I am not among them) report that the badger is more bluff than bite, however. It might not stop until it is an inch and three quarters from your ankles, but it will stop.

What looks menacing in a adult often seems merely amusing in a youngster. So it was with the infant badger I was now confronting toe to toe. Its funny black and white face, its short little ears, its short little legs, its enormous, bright, black eyes — all made it seem amusing, vulnerable, appealing.

The badger took no notice of me, although once or twice it almost bumped into me. It would come to the top of the road, flop onto its belly, tuck in its legs, and slide down the young grass into the ditch. When it had reached the bottom, it would flop about until it had found its balance again, right itself, scramble back up the bank, and slide down all over again. It looked as if it was having a wonderful time.

We humans, in our thirst for exotica, like to imagine that we alone have contrived aesthetic pleasures. But it is impossible to listen to a coyote singing at moonrise or to watch a flock of swallows on the wing or to encounter a young badger at play without believing that joy is as much a biological fact of life as any other.

I, at any rate, catching the mood of the badger, went on my way again with a skip and a hop.

I was at the Sunrise Prairie one windy afternoon, intent upon finding a particular flower, when I was startled by the bolting of a bird. I started, looked up to see a mourning dove fleeing to a telephone wire, and scarcely avoided crushing the two tiny white eggs resting in a makeshift grass receptacle at my feet. Because it was the middle of the day, the egg-sitter was probably the father.

In the marshes, the female blackbirds were on their impossible and nearly invisible nests among the rushes, and the male blackbirds were busy fending off every invader, friendly or dangerous.

It was the season of the year when the reptiles made themselves apparent. Coming down to the edge of a prairie pond at this time of year, one almost inevitably surprised a garter snake. If it was near enough to the water, it would slip in and disappear with astonishing speed, leaving not so much as a telltale ripple on the surface. If it was on higher ground, it would dart away into the undercover of mulch and hide there until the danger had passed. At the appearance of a human invader, the mud turtles that had been taking the sun would slide down from the half-submerged trunk of a willow tree into the murky cover of the waters, and the heads of the snapping turtles, barely visible at the center of the pond, would recede silently from view. The chatter of frogs and crickets would halt. A blackbird would take to the air and begin to scold. It was like a curtain suddenly crashing down on the drama.

A calf had just been born in the pasture across the way. It raised its head and seemed to be alive. Its mother licked it and tried to get it to stand. It wouldn't or couldn't. The mother cried to it. I went off to look at other things, and when I came back, the calf's mother had left it behind, and it seemed to be dead. The calf made a blue shadow on the hillside.

The lacy baskets of the tent caterpillars adorned the branches of every plum tree. The caterpillars were early, as everything was after the mild winter, and fewer of them had emerged than might have if the winter had been longer and colder. Tent caterpillar eggs need a good, hard, prolonged freezing to hatch best. If you leave some indoors where it is cozy all winter long, they will not hatch at all.

The tents of the caterpillars got bigger as the days passed and as the moth larvae grew. Each tent held many of them. In four to six weeks, the caterpillars would be mature, and they would leave the tent for solitary lives elsewhere. By and by, each of those that survived would make cocoons, and after another winter, the cocoons would emerge as moths, which would lay eggs. After still another winter had passed, there would be tents again.

But a great many of the caterpillars would not survive the birds, and perhaps the intervening years would be abnormally warm or abnormally cold and many of them would die of exposure.

In fields and along city streets wherever I looked, there were the carcasses of the birds that had not lived. The maggots had gotten into some of them, and those that had fallen prey to predators were remembered only because of the telltale clutches of feathers that remained here and there. Even now, death was always lurking in the shadows.

It was, at last, the time of the flowers. The open prairies bloomed with birds-foot violet, Missouri violet, northern bog violet, prairie smoke, golden Alexanders, lousewort, hoary puccoon, rue anemone, false rue anemone, false Solomon's seal, leadplant, wild strawberry, chokecherry and blue-eyed grass, among others.

From now until autumn, there would be every few days and then every day, a new kind of blossom on the prairie.

Excerpt from *Journal of a Prairie Year.* University of Minnesota Press, Minneapolis. Copyright © 1985 by the University of Minnesota.

Paul Gruchow was raised on a farm near Montevideo, educated at the University of Minnesota, and for the past decade has made his home at Worthington, Minnesota. He was a legislative aide, a radio news director, an editor of magazines and editor of a daily newspaper before he turned his attentions fulltime to writing. He is a regular columnist for *Minnesota Monthly* and publisher of *The Observer.* His books include *Journal of a Prairie Year; A Book of Chores* by Bob Artley, which he edited; and *The Necessity of Empty Places.* He began writing in order to discover what it is that attracts him so powerfully to the prairie landscape, and he continues to write in order to celebrate the majesty of all natural life.

David R. Harris

EARTH TONES

Prone I lay
   on lawn,
  head sideways,
    grass tickling eyeball,
  ear hard against earth,
     listening.

At first, nothing;
  well —
    wind soughs,
    leaves shoosh,
    branches *crik!* and rattle,
    jay squawks,
    squirrel chits,
    sparrow declares, "We're up! We're up! We're up!";
    distant lawn mower sputs and pouts;
    screen door slaps, bounces,
    far off child's voice shrills, "Bye!";
    tennies crackle gravel.

But underneath,
  from deep in earth,
   no murmurs:
  No moan, no scrape, no susurration of breath,
    no *puh-puh-puh* of engine
    that drives this planet
       nor
  throomp-bump! of heart that steadily beats and beats
        and beats.

Is Earth dead? Empty? Silenced?
    An egg unfertilized,
     a shell enclosing lifeless yolk?

Surely, sullen burblings should pop from lava
            in molten core,
    screaks scrape from tectonic plates
        as continents drift apart,
    grunts puff from rock powderized
        against harder stone.
    — At least, worms chewing, grass tendrils slithering,
            tree roots slurping.

Why only
    the *ump-ump!* of my own pulse
        echoing in my ear?

Then: *clop! clop!* a snort
        and whinny,
        and daughter's high clear voice
            from horseback:
    "Dad? Are you all right?
        You're so quiet."

"Yes — O yes!"

I heard the earth then sing.

David R. Harris is a member of Root River Poets of Rochester, Minnesota, and has taught such classes as freshman English and poetry writing at Rochester Community College during the past twenty years. He writes poetry, short stories, and musical comedy and has been previously published in *Streets and Towers,* an annual poetry magazine of which he is literary editor. He and his wife Judy have three children.

Steve Eide

SPRING RESUMÉ

My experience is extensive
regarding warming patterns and the
black return of silken feathered Starlings.
Starting at the bottom,
I've worked up
as mud scent loosens,
slippery through grass
into purple plaited Lilac air.
With no formal education,
I've had success breaking
winter's silver clouds and
the sure frozenness of water
to many pleated liquid calm.
I am flexible: Wrap me
in steel gray winter and
I am, going over, around, under,
gone like Houdini's song
until summer and
I'm ordered
absent.

THE EXECUTION OF ICE

Around the naked, thin island thickets,
from the white frosting of battered ice
and silver water segments,
steam alights to the sky's several blues,
smoking like a blindfolded man
as spring prepares the execution.

Steve Eide is a Minneapolis-based free-lance journalist with a B.A. in English Literature
from the University of Minnesota. He has written news and feature stories, essays and
book reviews for *Twin Cities Reader, City Pages, Minnesota Lawyer, Update, Minneapolis Sunday Tribune* and others. In the ten years he's been writing poetry, his credits
include *Loonfeather, The Great River Review* and *Update*.

Linda Essig

THE BULLDOG TRADITION

The feeling hits on weekends — especially weekends in the spring.

One Saturday in May as I left for the golf course, the neighborhood resembled an animated cartoon. Rakers moved as fast as the infamous Road Runner, window washers climbed ladders at speeds that would challenge Superman, and gardeners planted with the fury of Popeye after a gulp of spinach. I slouched in my seat as I drove past. A wave or a smile would have given me away, like a neon sign with the flashing message: *The occupant of this vehicle is going golfing.*

Attempting to shake the worthless feeling, I told myself that the windows were washed and the lawn raked. Actually, it had been power raked, hand raked, aerated, mowed, trimmed and fertilized. The result: faster growing grass, more work.

Throughout that afternoon my inner voice nagged, "Things look great outside the house, but what about inside?" The debate of cleaning versus relaxation traveled in my head, covering as much distance as my golf ball. My score, without whiffs, barely stayed in double figures — for nine holes.

Speaking of doubles, it's an accepted fact that there are only two things in life that are certainties: death and taxes. In Minnesota, however, there's a third: spring cleaning. If I were to rank the three — with last place going to the most dreaded — I'm not sure death would get that distinction. Minnesotans aren't pardoned from cleaning — only from relaxation. I've never heard anyone say, "It's time for spring golfing."

During my childhood, spring *and* fall signaled major cleaning. The unwritten law we lived by was: work equals worth. I'm having a hard time banishing that equation from my head. My parents believed in a quote by Thomas Jefferson, "It is while we are young that the habit of industry is formed. If not then, it never is afterwards."

I believe in a more contemporary quote, "What we grew up with, we learned; what we learned, we practiced; and what we practiced, we became." For me, that's work.

Most Minnesotans would concur. Living — being worthwhile — is measured by the work that we do, not by the fact that we exist.

I'm not saying work doesn't have its place. It just shouldn't be the only place there is. Sometimes, I lose sight of that.

When our son was confirmed, I got so caught up in cleaning and shopping that I never sat down and talked to him about the importance of this occasion in his life.

Last month I prepared for book club at my house by knocking down cobwebs and assembling a banquet instead of a simple snack. What I didn't take time to do was read the book we were discussing. When I go to extremes, I qualify as a "workaholic," and some day — having neglected my relationships — I may wake up with only myself for company.

Other Minnesotans travel along this same highway. Even social conversations steer our thinking. The question "What do you do for a living?" has become "What do you do?" The implication: you have to do something, or you wouldn't be living.

For me, work is so tied in with worth that taking a detour is difficult, and most Minnesotans follow the same life map. The statement, "I work twenty-four hours a day," is voiced so often it could be our state motto.

I don't work twenty-four hours a day, but some days when I'm depressed, I overcompensate — by working overtime — to prove I'm worthwhile. On those days, I start at seven, eat lunch at my desk and stay at my computer until after six. If I want to really prove something to myself, I make a huge dinner, do the laundry and go grocery shopping. If I still don't feel worthwhile, I start the next day's work.

Friends have different — but essentially the same — ways of proving their worth. Some have gardens big enough to put a dent in world hunger. After they spend hours growing their tomatoes, they spend hours giving them away — and then they pick apples at an orchard to supply their marathon bake-offs. There must be a special highway to heaven for people who "have fifteen pies in the freezer."

Because my friends do most of their gardening and pie baking on weekends, when I choose to get up late on Saturday and take in an afternoon matinee — or take the whole weekend off — I don't broadcast that information. But I don't keep the guilt to myself.

When my husband and I stayed at a motel to celebrate our anniversary, I spent two hours whining about how guilty I felt being away, doing nothing. He reminded me that we both worked hard and deserved time off.

My theory is different. On Memorial Day weekend I worked part of Friday evening and all day Saturday in preparation for a guilt-free holiday on Monday. I have to suffer a little first to justify relaxation.

Will my children have to deal with this syndrome? Since we carry everything from our family of origin with us, their heritage will be my work habits. Could I pass those habits on now and be rid of them? Last winter I wished that were the case.

My brother offered my husband and I a free trip to Hawaii because he couldn't go. For my husband there was no decision to be made, but for me there was a dilemma. I had committed myself to several important work projects during the time we'd be gone.

Since I feel less guilty if I'm talked into having fun, I polled several friends about my "predicament." After they all volunteered to go in my place, I started packing.

In Hawaii we met a young couple on a beach who had gotten off the freeway of life and were taking the scenic route. When my husband asked what they did, the man said, "We're doing it." That comment made me reflect on a trip to Colorado. The people we'd met there were laid back, semi-serious even when they were working.

Encounters like those validate the bumper sticker that declares: Survive Minnesota — the rest of the world is easy.

And my discussion with people across the state further confirms the bumper sticker philosophy. When I ask "What does being a worthwhile person mean?" I'm not surprised by the answers.

A Rochester friend says, "I'd feel more worthwhile if I wrote to my grandmother, kept a daily journal of my kids' activities and cleaned the bathroom sink." Another woman answers, "Doing what I enjoy doing, career-wise. And being a caretaker, meeting my family's needs."

From Spring Valley come similar comments, "Helping others and being able to support my family." And, "Feeling a part of the world with something of value to give back."

From Springfield: "You're worthwhile when you set your goals and achieve them. It's the good you have done." And, "It's giving of self, through helping others."

In every answer the words are different, but the message is the same: Being worthwhile means doing something.

In all fairness, one person did say, "We need to learn that simply *being* is worthwhile." (He's a psychiatrist who grew up in Europe.)

Others have shared his way of thinking, like the ancient Greeks. They placed true value on leisure. The idea of contemplation was bound up for them with the idea of leisure. Those who could contemplate were considered blessed and happy.

That belief is miles from the doctrine of the Protestant ethic, which was summarized in a sermon delivered in 1900: "Business is religion and religion is business."

The Protestant ethic can well be compared to the Minnesota work ethic. Minnesotans work hard and their work is important to them. They thrive on performing well, on being productive, and they suffer when they're not. It's been proven by productivity research here that about two-thirds of stress and dissatisfaction is linked to nonproductive behavior. There is great pride in this state in what working hard accomplishes.

I — and my friends and neighbors — belong in Minnesota. Our work attitudes qualify us as Minnesotans. We benefit from living in a state that borders on being neurotic about work. The consequences of growing up here are as close as the change in our pockets.

Minnesota and work are synonymous. Since we tend to live longer than any other Americans with the exception of Hawaiians, and consistently rank near the top in all major quality-of-life studies, working hard has its advantages.

Minnesota's work force is not only productive, it's successful. We rank number one on a per capita basis as the state that has produced the most new and fast-growing enterprises in the country. Even more important, those businesses have a better-than-average chance of survival.

New businesses, however, are not the only benefactors of our work force; established firms reap rewards also. A printer's promotion booklet listed as a reason for their competitive prices: "We still live by the old work ethic: a fair day's pay for a hard day's work."

Our work force is groomed by family training and educational opportunities. From its beginnings as a territory, education has been stressed. When Minnesota became a state in 1858, the University of Minnesota was already seven years old. And the Twin Cities area has the lowest high school dropout rate in the nation.

These graduates can expect to join a stable business world. In 1985, *Inc.* magazine rated Minnesota's "climate for small businesses" seventh-best in the nation. So the Control Data ad about our state is right on the mark: "Even at 20° below, we have a warm business climate."

Duluth residents delight in telling how — back in 1871 — they got into the seaport business ahead of nearby Superior, Wisconsin. Folks in Duluth had decided to dig a canal through the strip of land that separated their end of the harbor from the open waters of Lake Superior. Folks in Superior had been enjoying the competitive advantage provided by a natural opening to the lake. They took the matter to federal court and secured an injunction.

Unfortunately for Superior, the federal court was a great distance away — at St. Louis. Duluth partisans had stationed a spy there who telegraphed them the threatening news. When the U.S. marshal got off the train in Duluth with the court order, the city stalwarts, digging night and day, had finished the canal, and the first ship was already steaming into Duluth's end of the harbor.

In Duluth, where even the University's athletes are called Bulldogs, hanging in there is a tradition.

The bulldog tradition exists in workers all over the state. They have a "can-do" attitude, which extends into the workplace. In Minnesota — other than weather — work is the most talked about topic of conversation.

I asked a friend what she thought the term "Minnesota work ethic" meant. "I worked until midnight again last night," she said. "I *am* the Minnesota work ethic."

Linda Essig lives with her computer (and husband and sons) in Spring Valley, Minnesota. In addition to being part of the editing team of this book, she writes essays, short stories and articles. Some of her credits include *Weight Watchers Magazine, Growing Parent, Living With Teenagers* and *The Modern Woodmen.* Her philosophy, especially when applied to writing, is to approach life as if you were a sponge — absorb everything around you, then squeeze out what you need when you need it.

SUMMER

Garrison Keillor

from
LAKE WOBEGON DAYS

In winter, we sit in the house
Around a blazing fire.
In summer, we sit on the porch
Like birds on a telephone wire.

Society of summer evenings in Lake Wobegon was formal and genteel. We didn't bolt our food and jump up from the table but waited for the slowest eater, me, who hated all vegetables except pickles, and cleared the table, and two of us did dishes, a race between washer and wiper. By then, it was six o'clock. Children of age could go out bike-riding, the younger ones played in the yard. Mother and Dad worked in the yard, except Wednesday, which was prayer meeting, and then sat on the porch, and one by one we joined them.

The porch is about thirty feet long, almost the width of the house, and six feet, eight inches wide. The porch is enclosed with ten-foot-tall screens and we sit in old brown wicker chairs, rocker, couch, except me. I lie on the floor, feet to the house, and measure myself against that wonderful height. A six-eight person can pretty much write his own ticket.

"They say we're supposed to get some rain," Ralph said, stopping by our porch, "but then they've been saying that for a week." The grass is brown, and you can taste dust in your mouth. A cloud of dust boils up behind Mel's car when he comes with the mail, and then he doesn't stop at the mailbox. Not even a shopper today or the phone bill *(Who called Minneapolis last month? Three dollars! What do you think this is, the Ritz Hotel?)*. Not even a free pamphlet from Congressman Zwickey's office, something from the U.S.D.A. about keeping cool.

The dog days of August, they're called, but you get them in July, too, days when dogs camp under the porch where the dirt is cool and damp or lie panting in the shade, big grins on their faces. Good old Buster. Phyllis and I trimmed him one afternoon and kept trimming until we got him trimmed all even, he was clipped down to the stubble. A dog heinie. He seemed grateful. We ran the hose on him and he lay in the sun and got a dog tan.

Nobody in this family lies in the sun. You work in the sun, you lie in the shade. We don't have air-conditioning, of course. "If you'd work up a little sweat out there, the shade ought to feel good enough for you," is Dad's thinking. Air-conditioning is for the weak and indolent. This isn't the Ritz, you know. Be thankful for a little breeze.

It was luxuries like A/C that brought down the Roman Empire. With A/C, their windows were shut, they couldn't hear the barbarians coming. *Decadence:* we're on the verge of it, one wrong move and *k-shoom!* the fat man sits on your teeter-totter. You get A/C and the next day Mom leaves the house in a skin-tight dress, holding a cigarette and a glass of gin, walking an ocelot on a leash.

What about the Ingqvists, they have air-conditioning.

We're not the Ingqvists.

What about Fr. Emil?

He has hay fever.

Father's hay fever was so bad last summer, he could hardly breathe. His face was puffy, he went around with a hanky in his hand. He went to the North Shore for some relief in August, but one week alone with all that scenery was all he could bear. So he's got an immense NorthernAire in his bedroom window and he lives up there.

It was when Mrs. Hoglund got one that people talked. There was nothing wrong with her, so who did she think she was? She said she got it for Janice who broke out in heat rash, but Janice only visited for a week or two and always in June. "Well, it was probably a mistake," Mrs. Hoglund said, "but as long as I have it, I might as well get the use of it." So we'd sit on our porch on an August evening, quietly perspiring, and hear her machine humming next door. If only there were a way to connect air-conditioning to health or education. An article in the *Digest:* "Air-Conditioning: Man's New Weapon Against Malaria." COMFORTABLE CHILDREN SCORE HIGH IN SCHOOL, STU-DIES SHOW — KEEPING COOL ALSO CUTS CASES OF POLIO, SAYS DR. But school is out, and Mother thinks air-conditioning causes colds. When I remark on the heat, she simply says, "Make the best of it. Life is what you make it." Her answer to any complaint without specific symptoms. "Life is what you make it."

I feel that the saying "Life is what you make it" points directly *toward* air-conditioning. Mrs. Hoglund is making the best of it, obviously. She is sitting and enjoying a fine program on television (which we don't have either) and is cool as a cucumber.

"We could try having an air conditioner and see if we like it, and if we don't, we can send it back."

I sit, all hot and bothered, suffering, and mention this. Mother says, "Go outside. Do something. Take your mind off it." But outside is not the answer. I want to be inside with cold air blowing at me. I've *been* outside in the garden working. The rule around here is that you finish your work first before you take off and play, which means that I waste the cool of the morning slaving over vegetables I don't like, and when I'm finally free to take off, it's too hot to do much. I get my golf club, a mashie niblick, out of the garage and play an imaginary game I invented, called Championship Golf: wherever I hit the ball, wherever it stops, that's where the hole is. I'm the champion, but it's boring to be so good, and it's hot. I sit under a tree with two other kids, talking about what we would do if we had a million dollars. I would buy a large cool house with a swimming pool and hire some servants. Bringing me glasses of cold nectar is what they would do, and cranking up the air conditioner.

Despite the heat and no rain, gardens come on like gangbusters, faster than we can haul in the stuff and give it away. Ralph sells no produce in July and August, not an ounce. Cans of Libby's tomatoes gather dust on his shelves. Tomatoes are free for the asking, sacks of tomatoes are thrust on you after church.

Nothing has changed in the garden since then.

Slaving in her half-acre spread, August 1984, Mrs. Luger doesn't recall the garden fever that hit her and the Mister last winter when months of cold weather set them off on a seed binge, and they careened through the catalog like submarine sailors on shore leave, grabbing everything in sight.

By May 1, twenty little tomato plants in sawed-off milk cartons had taken over the kitchen dinette. Two large boxes from Gurney's cooled their heels on the chairs. Mr. Peterson and his Allis-Chalmers plowed the half-acre on his plowing route through town, and Mr. Luger worked it with a rake, busting up the big clods, making a flat brown table. May Day dawned warm and sunny, and the two veterans nodded at each other over morning coffee. It was V-Day.

By July, Mr. and Mrs. started to feel they'd set something in motion back there that was getting out of hand, and now, late July and August, the glacier is moving in on them for good. The pressure cooker has been running full blast for days, Ralph is out of Kerr lids, but vegetables fill up the fridge, the kitchen counter — quarts of tomatoes have been canned, still more tomatoes move in. The Mister reaches for the razor in the morning, he picks up a cucumber. Pick up the paper, underneath it are three zucchini. They crawled in under there to get some shade, catch a few Zs, maybe read the comics. Pumpkins are moving in to live with them. At night they check the bed for kohlrabi. Turn out the lights, they hear rustling noises downstairs: a gang of cauliflower trying the back door. Go to sleep, dream about watermelon vines reaching out and wrapping their spiny little fingers around your neck, the Big Berthas, the forty-pounders. Those cantaloupe they planted, the Dauntless Dukes: why plant twelve hills? why not two?

"I like to have extra just in case and also it's nice to have some to give away," says Mrs. Luger, her hair melted to her head from an afternoon of canning. *But everyone else has some to give away.*

Back in April, she'd have killed for a tomato. Not the imported store tomatoes that were strip-mined in Texas, but fresh garden tomatoes that taste like tomatoes. That's how my mother felt, too, back then in my youth, so in May she set out thirty or forty tomato plants to satisfy our tomato lust and now, going into August, fresh tomatoes are no more rare or wonderful than rocks, each of us has eaten a bushel of them and there are plenty left where those came from.

One night, she and I snuck over to the Tollefsons' after their lights went out and left a half-bushel of tomatoes on their back step.

On this morning in August when I am thirteen, it's hot by ten o'clock. I poked along over the Post Toasties as long as I could, then my mother sent me out to pick tomatoes. Rudy and Phyllis were already out there. I picked one and threw it at a crab apple tree. It made a good *splat.* The tree was full of little crab apples we'd have to deal with eventually, and a few of them fell. My brother and sister stood up and looked: what did you *do?* we're gonna tell.

I picked the biggest tomato I saw and took out a few more crab apples. Then I threw a tomato at my brother. He whipped one back at me. We ducked down by the vines, heaving tomatoes at each other. My sister, who was a good person, said, "You're going to get it." She bent over and kept on picking.

What a target! She was seventeen, a girl with big hips, and bending over, she looked like the side of a barn.

I picked up a tomato so big it sat on the ground. It looked like it had sat there for a week. The underside was brown. Small white worms lived in it. It was very juicy. I had to handle it carefully to keep from spilling it on myself. I stood up and took aim, and went into the wind-up, when my mother at the kitchen window called my name in a sharp voice. I had to decide quickly. I decided.

A rotten Big Boy hitting the target is a memorable sound. Like a fat man doing a bellyflop, and followed by a whoop and a yell from the tomatoee. She came after me faster than I knew she could run, and I took off for the house, but she grabbed my shirt and was about to brain me when Mother yelled "Phyllis!" and my sister, who was a good person, obeyed and let go and burst into tears. I guess she knew that the pleasure of obedience is pretty thin compared to the pleasure of hearing a rotten tomato hit someone in the rear end.

"Look at what he did!" she said, but Mother just said that that was enough of *that* and to get back to work. That was fine with me. Later Phyllis caught me coming out of the bathroom and pinched me. In my baby picture, still displayed on the piano, she held me on her lap and looked down at me with pure devotion. I couldn't help telling her how much her attitude had changed. I told her not to be so unhappy. "Life is what you make it," I said. "You should get out and enjoy yourself more." As I said it, I jumped back in the bathroom and locked the door. She pounded on it, then pretended to go downstairs, but I could tell fake footsteps and I stayed put. "I can hear you breathing," I said. I stayed put for all of one *Reader's Digest* and part of another. A door slammed downstairs. My mother called my name. I yelled for help. She came upstairs. "She's hiding. She's after me," I said. "Don't be silly," Mother said, "there's nobody here but me."

From *Lake Wobegon Days*, by Garrison Keillor. Copyright © Garrison Keillor, 1985. Reprinted by permission of Viking Penguin, Inc.

Garrison Keillor was born in Anoka, Minnesota, graduated from the University of Minnesota, and lives in St. Paul. Every Saturday evening he performs on "A Prairie Home Companion" which is broadcast by the American Public Radio network. His first book, *Happy to Be Here*, was published in 1982. *Lake Wobegon Days*, published in 1985, became a bestseller and brought national attention to Keillor and the mythical Minnesota town where "All the men are strong, the women good-looking, and the children above average."

Myron Bietz

FROM THE FROZEN NORTH

45N 92.45W
3 August 3906

Fr. Juan Mohamet-Jones, Director
Department of Anthropology
San Guevera University
Nuevo Fidelia, Hispaniola

Honored Director:

Since my last report from the Manna/Soda site, we have moved
our camp two kilometers eastward, eliminating the daily journey to
our new dig and allowing maximum work hours in the waning light.
The cold grows intense; wind-driven ice crystals penetrate robes and
sting ankles. But the personal discomfort is nothing compared to our
frustration as we watch excavations drift over. We have another week
or ten days at best before we must abandon our efforts for the
season, even though we are so tantalizingly close to meeting our
goal of establishing the long-sought link between the ancient lake-
dwellers of this area and the Mizaseebee tribes to the south. We will
continue, Gods willing, as long as we are able. When progress is no
longer possible, we will begin the 900 kilometer trek across the ice

floes to the great arch at San Luis, then southward to Nuevo Orlean, and finally home.

Although we have concentrated our efforts on the new dig, two additional discoveries at the first site have supported speculation about the people who built and used the structure. You will recall that we were unable to penetrate more than two levels below the ice surface, though shaft markings indicate another fifty levels to a crystal court beneath. You can be assured that we will seek additional equipment and personnel to continue our work there next season. The two new artifacts, both found in a waste bin, will certainly support the request.

The first object is a torn admission ticket. One can easily infer the ritual: The believer, having purchased his passage, ascends to the tower's summit, rends his ticket, and — amid chants and incantations — leaps to his eternal reward.

Dr. Noam Qaddafi-Sanchez, the expedition philologist, is intrigued by the markings on the ticket. He believes that "IDS" is a variant name of the ancient Idegosuperego trinity. Additional research is called for. Correlation of findings with elements of later belief systems will occupy numerous post-doctoral studies.

The second object, potentially more significant, is a crumpled container with the sign of the arches on its side! This is our first concrete evidence of Archism at so extreme a latitude. At the very least, it indicates visits by Mizaseebee missionaries. We feel that continued digging will reveal additional links between Archism and Idism (as we have come to call the religion of the lake-dwellers). We may, with persistence and the Gods' blessings, uncover a temple of the golden arches similar to the one found near the great arch at San Luis.

We have carefully preserved the container and will bring it to Nuevo Fidelio for laboratory study. It is nearly boat-shaped with a grease-stained interior. Where it might have sailed, literally or figuratively, and what cargo it might have carried, remain mysteries.

But I digress. My purpose in this report is to describe progress at our second dig.

Our earliest indication of a structure was a huge, nearly circular depression. For reasons not yet clear, the ice is thinner and much less densely packed here than at first site. When test borings revealed solid edges and a hollow center, we decided to dig.

As work progressed, we began to realize the potential significance of our find. This was a temple of unusual proportions. Tiers of seats still surround and face the central pit. At one time scores of thousands must have worshipped here!

At first we assumed an open-air structure, much like the amphitheaters of ancient Greece. But then we discovered traces of a flexible fabric covering. Remaining portions had been patched and the patches repatched. How it remained in place is still uncertain. Clearly though, the lake dwellers protected their rituals from the elements and hid them from prying or unworthy eyes.

Around the inner circumference of the building but outside the seating area were the usual facilities for crowds: ramps and stairways, segregated relief stations, multiple portals and bazaars. At one bazaar were long, thin-skinned inflatables with the appearance of chubby swords. Our behavioral expert, Dr. Sigmund Garcia-Skinner, has developed two hypotheses concerning them. In the first the inflatables are surrogate weapons, used to release pent-up hostilities without inflicting physical damage. The second hypothesis holds that the inflatables are not swords at all but personal, portable phalli, repeating the image of the giant IDS structure to the west.

A series of rooms at a lower level — surprisingly free of ice and therefore accessible — provide new riddles. Hooks and metal closets suggest that these rooms were once used as costume areas. In the larger rooms the closets are empty. But on a central rack we found a variety of strap-on underpinnings, padding mostly, that must have been used to enhance the physical features of the wearers. Considering the great distances from the seating areas to the pit, it is likely that priests and dancers wore the pads under their robes in order to be more easily seen by the assembled worshippers. The only other object in the room was a thick-skinned bladder which, when inflated, must have had the appearance of a large brown egg. You can imagine the theories Garcia-Skinner set forth after finding such an item in this womb-like structure!

In a smaller costume room nearby we found the only examples of priestly garb. The robes appeared to be fashioned from the skins of animals — perhaps polar beasts, but darker. Head coverings sprouted pairs of animal horns, although no animal masks could be found. These items seem consistent with our knowledge of the ancient shamans. A huge wooden sword and shield add yet another dimension to the riddle of the inflatables.

I have delayed telling you of our most exciting find. A new link to Archism is almost certain! In a booth on the exterior of the structure we found an unused quantity of tickets, each bearing the marking "TWINS." A sports-history buff in our party, Dr. Billy

Martinez-Pohlad, has suggested that this could be a reference to the Tampa Twins of beisbol fame. It is my belief, however, that the reference is to the twin arches. Somewhere in that pit, below the tons of pack ice, upright arches will be found.

Please convey greetings to families and colleagues, telling them that we are safe and well. If the Gods permit, we may be able to work another two weeks. If not, we will go by sled-train to San Luis, thence by boat to Nuevo Orlean and home.

In fidelitas,

/s/

Manuel Steger-Peary, O.S.G., Commanding
Northern Glacial Expedition

Myron Bietz lives in Rochester, Minnesota, and is a fan of speculative fiction, a student and teacher, an amateur photographer and a peace activist. His writing has appeared in professional journals and religious magazines. He hopes to be an archaeologist in his next incarnation.

Karen Sandberg

GREEN

Green
as seaweed,
the Swiss Chard
ripples and curves
under tap water,
next the curly
lettuce crinkles.
I feast my eyes
on curliques
of summer,
first garden harvest.
Aging
ignites the magic
of seed in soil
to reach the sun.
I see myself,
through the years,
hair as crinkly
as white lettuce,
rejoicing in each year's
new batch
of curving chard,
regimented beans,
prolific zucchini.
An outrageous old woman
dancing
with the hot tomatoes.

LILIES

From decay spring
pale lilies, tingling
in the northern sun,
their silent chimes
flicker in summer stillness.

The woodland floor reverberates
in lily light.
The loon calls, drifting away.
Waves, sun dipped, ripple to shore.
The fragrance of earth rises.

Northern summer enchants the mind,
loosens the grip of heartache
in the pristine clarity
of pale lilies,
reverberating
stillness
in green water light.

Karen Sandberg makes her living as a nurse at Rochester Methodist Hospital, but she likes to think that her real vocation is writing, which she returned to six years ago. Her first published poem appeared in the 1986 *Streets and Towers*. She combines writing with raising two large teenage sons and a small cat, a heady mix.

Jonathan Borden

SUNDAY AFTERNOON AT THE TRACK

When our combined income swung dangerously low, Kirsten and I drove out of the city onto the prairie where the Minnesota River meanders like a snake on glass. It was the first Sunday of thoroughbred horse racing at Minnesota's new and only track. Out in the open farmland, our dove-gray junker had a little trouble with the early afternoon heat on this last day of June. The corn was knee high. The sky was a powdery blue, with huge motionless clouds heaped on the horizon like the empty thought balloons of cartoon giants asleep in the earth.

We'd never been to a racetrack, but we'd read the newspaper hoopla promoting the delights of pari-mutuel betting and the family fun of a day at the races. Frequent editorials extolled the authorities for preventing the "criminal element" from oozing into Canterbury Downs. There wasn't any nearby community called Canterbury, but the racetrack developers had held a contest to name the place, and you can trust a contest to trot out the puns. Another contest, at the Como Park Zoo in St. Paul, settled on the name Perry Como for a newborn penguin.

"Too bad about keeping out the sleaze element," Kirsten said. "The whole thing's beginning to sound like a church bazaar."

We swung off the cracked old highway onto one of the smooth new approaches to the racetrack. We could see the grandstand, its creamy walls and red roofs with turrets and pennons, and the matching barns and stables beyond, all rising from the corn fields like a fairyland chateau — or, seen through the green plastic visor of my straw fedora, like Dorothy's view of the Emerald City of Oz. Walking through the vast parking lot and noticing that the grandstand, with its back to the afternoon sun, threw shade over the crowd, I regretted that hat. It was strictly hayseed.

"Wear it already," Kirsten said. "Look what happened to Vincent Van Gogh. Running around in the midday sun on the south of France, painting three or four masterpieces a day, he fried his brains without a hat." She wasn't wearing a hat, though, and her long hair glowed in the sun like dark honey.

The grandstand was air-conditioned but packed with feverish bettors. We went outside onto the asphalt apron sloping down to the finish line. People were standing around or sitting in their folding lawn chairs, a swaying field of pale colors, with a few Hawaiian shirts, some of the women in floppy-brimmed straw hats and some of the men in straw boaters or Panama hats — no green visors. They were facing the track to watch the changing odds on the tote board. There was hardly room to move.

We stepped back inside into the air conditioning and caught the fourth race on one of the television monitors hanging from the ceiling. Only three horses were running on the screen. A drunk was yelling advice to the monitor. He stood sideways, dropped a shoulder like Elvis Presley at a song's climax, and scowled up and screamed. When the horses hit the homestretch, the groups under the monitors roared. Then they rushed back to the betting windows. A voice from the loudspeakers anounced that at the last minute a horse had been scratched at the starting gate, on orders of the track veterinarian, and state law didn't allow show bets with fewer than five horses in a race. The fourth horse had lost its bridle just after starting and had dropped out. All show bets were canceled and would be refunded. The mob sent up a few baffled squawks and went on milling at the windows.

"It's late night at the airport, just before the bombs hit," Kirsten said.

We went outside again and worked our way down through the lawn chairs to the track. The horses had run on past the finish line and were now coming back to a semicircular ring beside the track. The dull brown dirt of the track was dry and crumbly. It was rated fast that day. I loved the soft thudding of hoofs. The jockeys dismounted and weighed in, holding their saddles. Kirsten was fascinated by their lean, deeply creased faces.

"None of them are smiling," she said. "You notice?"

"That's because jockeys don't race with their false teeth in," I said, vaguely remembering a scrap of possibly wrong information. "They might lose them on a jolt, or swallow them."

"They all have false teeth?"

"Lots of spills. Rough sport."

The jockeys disappeared down a tunnel under the grandstand, and the horses were walked back up the track to the barn. They passed the horses for the next race coming single file in a procession, led by a red-jacketed attendant on a bored gray horse, along the track and then up a narrow lane with a white wooden fence around behind the grandstand to the paddock — the saddling stalls and a parade ring. The horses, brown or bay, glossy in the sunshine, were maiden fillies three- or four-years-old, according to the program. None of them had won a race yet. Some of them yanked their heads away from the grooms holding their bridles, and one danced around sideways. Those looked like pests to me. I liked a brown filly that looked straight ahead with an air of great concentration. They trooped into the numbered paddock stalls for saddling. My favorite was number four, Reason Within.

Kirsten liked Ameca J., the most likely to win, according to the program's estimated odds of six to five. I checked the odds for Reason Within: fifteen to one. Pretty hopeless. "These are the morning-line odds," I said. "They're just guesses by a track handicapper. What's he know? Anyway, this is pari-mutuel betting. The final payoff odds change depending on how people bet. Reason Within looks okay to me."

"Ameca J.," Kirsten said.

The jockeys mounted, and the grooms led them down the fenced lane to the track for the post parade. We found a place to watch near the finish line. The jockeys limbered up their horses in front of the starting gate, on the far side of the track for this race. We couldn't see the horses' legs because of the track rail, and at that distance the horses seemed to glide back and forth.

"They look like water striders on a pond," Kirsten said, "or flies on a glass of lemonade."

We weren't betting yet. We wanted to scope out the setup first. Ameca J., Kirsten's favorite, came in second, and my Reason Within trailed about twenty lengths behind. I didn't think Reason Within had any idea why she was out there this pleasant June afternoon.

In the next race, still not betting, we both liked a roan named Icecatrope, who took the lead, kept it, and won by six lengths. Then we went for Mae Cry, who finished second. On the next race, we couldn't make up our minds over a couple of bays, Wee Irish Lass and Smooth Rib, until we saw them on their way to the track. Something about Smooth Rib's jaunty walk looked right, and her jockey had the highest standing at the track so far. Smooth Rib won. All this time, we'd been too cautious to bet our slim stake, but we'd been checking our choices against the predictions in the newspaper, and we were doing a little better than those guys.

We were waiting for the ninth race, the City of St. Paul Stakes, for three-year-olds and up. The consensus of the newspaper handicappers was that Plaza Star would win, followed by Manantial and Ismore. We had half an hour to talk it over, so we sat on a grass embankment and had a picnic of laughing-cow cheese and bock beer we'd brought in a cooler. We got into an awful argument. My theory was that Ismore would win.

"This guy in the paper thinks Plaza Star's the best bet because he won in Omaha last week," I said. "But Ismore won his last race, too, and with the same jockey, Montoya." I showed her the *Daily Racing Form*, which I'd sweated to smudges. "He's come in first, second, or third in all his last seven races, at different tracks since December."

"Why not go with this other guy favoring Manantial?" Kirsten suggested.

"For one thing, that guy's only guessed one winner so far all day in eight races," I said. "What's he know? Even this guy who's for Plaza Star thinks Manantial's over the hill. Besides, the more people who vote for Manantial and Plaza Star, the more we'll win on Ismore."

"Leif, it's called betting, not voting."

We were still bickering over the bet at the paddock as we watched them saddle up and walk around the parade ring with the intense jockeys aboard. Manantial was a big and powerful chestnut. He was seven years old and wasn't showing a lot of enthusiasm. Plaza Star looked sleepy. Ismore was a sleek five-year-old bay with fiery eyes and rippling muscles, not muscles all bunched and defined like a weight lifter's, but smooth and tireless as a farm boy's. One of the horses looked so coked up he'd run sideways, and another was so blissed out he probably couldn't have beaten Reason Within.

The upshot was we bet twenty dollars on Ismore to win and another twenty to show, as a covering bet in case he didn't win but was second or third. Kirsten was arguing to bet another twenty dollars on Manantial to place, because he'd been doing a lot of running second lately. I convinced her we'd be better off rooting for a single horse, so as not to jam our vibes — a dumb idea. She was steamed, I guess.

The race was a mile and a sixteenth, a little more than once around the track, so the starting gate was rolled out onto the stretch not far from where we were, up the track away from the grandstand. They loaded up the eight horses one by one. Ismore was number six, the sixth horse from the rail. His jockey would have to start fast and work him over near the rail quickly, before they went into the first turn. As soon as the last horse was into its gate stall, they took off. Ismore seemed to stumble behind the others.

The starting gate was in the way, so I watched the first turn on a television monitor behind us. The screen outdoors was faint, and I couldn't make out Ismore's colors, aqua with green diamonds. Over the loudspeakers, the announcer, in his clipped unemotional voice, called off the horses' positions. Ismore was far behind. After the knot of horses ran past, the monitor screen showed empty track for a moment, and then Ismore went tearing by alone. Kirsten snapped her bright blue eyes at me.

"Still plenty of time," I said.

Just before the second turn, the last turn, Ismore caught up and cruised around the outside and, coming off the turn, cut through the pack. The jockey gave him a few whacks, and Ismore swung into that elastic, impossible stretch of an all-out effort. He passed the lead, Plaza Star, right in front of us, his hoofs consuming the track in a thunderous rush. I can see him like a snapshot with all the motion in it. Manantial was gaining on him when they swept out of our view. The crowd was wild. Then we could see the first horses beyond the finish line, the jockeys rising out of their saddles and slowing down. The loudspeakers crisply announced Ismore first, Manantial second, and Dirty Bird third. Kirsten was jumping up and down, and I have to admit I'd given a cheer when Ismore took the lead.

We waited smugly to hear the final odds and payoffs. On a bench nearby, two guys were hunched over a *Racing Form*. One of them, a large beefy guy, was watching a monitor screen through binoculars. The other was saying something. The beefy guy lowered his binoculars and turned to his friend and shrieked, "Nobody cares what you bet on! Can't you get that through your head?"

The payoffs went up on the monitors. Ismore paid ten dollars to win and three-twenty to show. I took our ticket over to the windows and collected a hundred and thirty-two dollars. "That's why they're called *wind*ows," I said.

We left right away, to avoid the rush after the next race and get me to St. Paul in time for my job tending bar at O'Shaughnessy's Bar and Grill. After we'd bumped along the old highway awhile, Kirsten said, "If we'd bet twenty dollars on Manantial to place, we'd have cleared another twenty-two dollars."

Neither of us said anything for a few miles. My mind wandered across the fields and train tracks and grain elevators and junkyards while I stared straight ahead, automatically correcting the car's drift to the left. "I can't stop thinking about the races," I said. "All I have to do is close my eyes, and I see the horses running."

"You've come down with a case of Preteen Girl Syndrome," she said.

A few days later, Kirsten took off for Mexico with a friend. Her note didn't say who the friend was. I don't know whether to keep her things the way she left them or get jealous and hate all her stuff. I've been to the track a few more times. You pick up a lot of tips working in a bar. They say it's bad luck to mention how your bets are going, but I'm doing okay.

Jonathan Borden, of Minneapolis, Minnesota, has had a poem accepted by *Rolling Stone.* The earlier adventures of Leif and Kirsten appeared in the *Lake Street Review* and *City Pages.*

Marilyn J. Boe

PICKING BLUEBERRIES

Don't let anyone tell you it's fun. Don't get
nipped with nostalgia unless you're talking about
that big, cut glass bowl of dew drenched berries
in the center of Aunt Millie's farm table, next
to a stack of help-yourself bowls, creamer of
the thickest gold from the top of the separator,
and a sugar jar holding a fat spoon.

My parent's idea of enjoying blueberries was to
go out and pick them, all of us together inside
northern Minnesota woods with tin pails and orders
to bring them back full.

This was suffering for prime time news, if TV
had been born. Mosquitoes bit me ragged, sunshine
burned, humidity rose from soggy ground slippery
enough to send me sailing across spongy soil into
the arms of poison ivy.

I could have handled this if the reward was
my own bowl of berries, but all of mine, all of
theirs disappeared inside canning jars, drowned,
turned small and purple, the sunshine cooked out
of them, sealed with a stern twist of the Mason
cap, carried downstairs to serve time on a dark
shelf in the basement.

Like jewels in a vault, they were counted,
saved, to be brought up later as a special treat
for company I cannot remember ever coming.

GREAT BLUE HERONS

From an island
in Prior Lake,
the blue robed choir
rises in unison,
stretches angel wings,
trailing legs,
like rakes.

I look up
from my boat, see them
gather the sunset
around them
like a magician's cape,
swoop to the shoreline,
disappear.

In dim light, I see
blue umbrellas
neatly folded,
stuck in the sand.

Marilyn J. Boe lives in Bloomington, Minnesota, with her husband, Bill. Her poetry credits include *Milkweed Chronicle, Loonfeather, Whittier Globe, Sing Heavenly Muse!* and *Passages North.* She won the 1986 poetry contest sponsored by the St. Paul chapter of the American Association of University Women. In addition, she has completed a book-length manuscript of poetry entitled *Everlasting Fielder* and has another in progress under the working title *An Older Woman Looking Back At Me.*

Jon Hassler

ANNIVERSARY

I am home from the drugstore with the Sunday paper and a dozen ballpoint pens, all of them red. I leave the paper in the living room for Donna, and I am halfway up the stairs to my den when I suddenly realize that today is an anniversary. I return to the kitchen and pour two glassses of sherry. On this date ten years ago, my wife and I and eleven hundred other persons filed into the University of Minnesota football stadium and were given, with a full measure of blessings and addresses, our degrees. We both were twenty-two at the time. The principal speaker was a bishop who said that life was short.

Carrying the two wineglasses, I step out the back door into the sunshine. Robbie, eight, is golfing across the lawn with my putter, digging up grass as he goes along. Donna is on her knees in the garden, loosening the soil around the rosebushes.

"What? Ten years?" says Donna. "I can't believe it." She smiles and sits back on her heels and takes the glass in her large, dirty garden glove. As we toast a number of things, including my ten years as a high-school teacher, a warm June breeze stirs her red hair and uncovers at the temples a trace of gray. Life is short, said the bishop.

"We will go out to dinner," I announce. "After I finish my schoolwork, you and Robbie and I will go someplace for a festive dinner."

"Don't tell me you're planning to spend the day in the den," says Donna. "Sunday is no day for correcting papers."

"Final grades are due in the office tomorrow morning. My brief case is full of the scraps of the school year. Odds and ends."

We toast odds and ends, then Donna picks a blossom from the Flaming Peace rosebush and hands it to me. It has a long, thorny stem. Robbie joins us and I give him a sip of sherry, which he spits on the grass.

"Make reservations for three at some fancy place," I tell Donna. "We're stepping out when my work is done."

Upstairs in my den, I set the bottle of sherry on the window sill and I hang the rose by its thorns in the burlap draperies. It is a small blossom, unfurling from a tomato-colored bud. My window overlooks the garden, and as I crank it open Donna calls up to me, "Promise you won't be up there for the rest of the day."

I have never known Donna to be jealous of another woman, but I have at times a great appetite for solitude, and she is jealous of this room in which I find it. Once while working on my thesis, I spent fourteen days and nights in here, emerging only for sandwiches and a bath or two, and she never got over it. She said life was passing me by. And one day last winter, designing a new syllabus, I came in here and worked for twenty-two straight hours, and she broke down and wept. She said her mother had warned her about men who were consumed by their work.

I settle into my deep leather chair and open my brief case. It is full of quizzes, exams, themes, term papers and office mail — everything I was too busy to read when it first crossed my desk at school. Some of it goes back several months. I reach in and pull out a paper at random. It is an essay by Becky Burke titled "My Father."

Becky writes with a backward slant and she misspells all but the simplest words. She says here that she loves her father. "He has old fashion ideas," she writes, "and he argues with the length of my skirts but he is patient and he has a sence of humer." She tells of how he used to take her every summer to a "rodio." But now her father is not well. He has been in the hospital for six weeks. Becky fears he will die.

I want to write something tender in the margin, but if I am to read everything in my brief case this afternoon, I must be off to a quick start. With my red pen I write, "Proofread!" across the top of the paper, and I give her a C. By English Department standards a C is too generous for spelling like Becky's, but I cannot give a girl with a dying father a D.

A sudden cold wind springs through the window, billowing the draperies. Clouds cover the sun and the room darkens. Cranking the window shut, I see a flock of geese flying south — the wrong direction for June.

Next I read a letter from Dale Wood, president of the teachers' union. He wants me to serve for a year as union griever. Although I pay my dues, I am not much of a union man. I lost my enthusiasm years ago when the union went to court to defend a junior-high drama coach who undressed on stage. (Academic freedom, claimed the union; but the judge said nonsense and sent the drama coach somewhere for observation.) Yet Dale Wood has been a friend of mine for a long time. When we golf together he tells hilarious stories. In the margin of the letter I print, in red: "OKAY, ONE YEAR ONLY."

My red ink does not glisten as it should. I try the other pens I bought this morning, but none is any fresher. I have been sold a dozen dry pens. In my desk I have blue and black pens, but I will not use them. In my ten years of teaching, I have learned to understand the power of red ink. Red is alarming, decisive. Red puts everything else in the background. When I hand back a student's paper my red ink leaps out at him, and everything he wrote in blue ink has turned insignificant, powerless, faint. Red has the same effect with letters and memos. When I print my response in red it looks, no matter how innocuous the words, like a shout. If I leave my mark in this world, it will be a red mark. Red has force. But today my lettering is pale. It seems to fade before my eyes.

The wind grows stronger. Donna calls to me from the bottom of the stairs. She says she is going to take Robbie to his driving lesson and they will return in an hour. For a moment I am puzzled. Robbie is eight; he does not drive. She must mean she is taking him to the driving range. She must be bored.

"It's awfully windy for driving golf balls," I call to her, but she is gone. I hear the car drive away.

Another letter. This one too is from Dale Wood. Is this his idea of a joke? He writes, "You have doubtless received a letter of official thanks from the union office, but let me add my personal note of gratitude for the way you handled your job as griever these past several years. I know it's never any easy job...." My pen is poised but I can think of nothing to print in the margin. Sometimes Dale tries hard for a joke. There is nothing harder to respond to than a poor joke. I set his letter aside.

Next in my brief case I find an ad from the publishers of my American-literature text. It says that the new edition, soon to appear, will contain nothing earlier than *Leaves of Grass*. *Walden* will be replaced by a report from the National Ecology Council, and *Huckleberry Finn* by an assortment of comic strips. The book is to be called *Superlit*. I write "Supertrash" across the ad and drop it into the wastebasket. I pour myself another glass of sherry. It is the color of a rosebud, and smooth.

Donna calls up the stairs: "I am not feeling well." Her voice is husky.

"Are you back already?" I ask.

"I believe I'll lie down."

"Fine, Donna. Lie down. Where is Robbie?"

"Rob is over at Angeline's. I'm sure I'll be all right if I lie down."

"Angeline's? Who is Angeline?"

There is a trace of steam on the window. I wipe it off and look down at the garden. The Flaming Peace petals are drifting to the ground. Well, it has never been a hardy bush. To get it started, Donna nursed it through four summers without blossoms, and to this day it is easily discouraged by a sudden cold snap or a sharp wind.

I resume reading. This is Alvin Turvig's essay on "Memories." Who is Alvin Turvig? I have never heard of Alvin Turvig. He writes, "My earliest memory is of my family watching, on TV, Richard Nixon's departure from the White House." I read no further. In red I print, "Yours must be the shortest memory in Adams High School," and I move on.

Here is a letter from Cletus Hamburger, who sells insurance in St. Paul. Cletus is the only college classmate I still correspond with. In this letter he seems to be straining, like Dale Wood, to make a joke. He says that he is retiring from the insurance business. He says that he and his wife from now on will spend their winters in El Paso. "Why don't you and Donna join us?" he writes. As I said before, a poor joke leaves me with no reply. I put a red question mark in the margin.

I take a sip of sherry and feel hairs or threads on my lip. Holding the glass up to the light, I pick from the rim the strands of a cobweb. There are raindrops on the window. Outside, a robin with an ebony eye stands on an elm twig, glancing nervously about him at the leaves shaken by the rain. The leaves of the tree are yellow. Can my elm be dying?

Another paper, this one by Peter Turvig. *Peter* Turvig? Who are these Turvigs? He writes, "My Uncle Alvin, who can remember all the way back to the early '70s, is home on vacation. Yesterday he taught me how to fix the brakes on my bike. He goes back to work next week. He is on the staff of the U.S. Embassy in the Republic of Antarctica." This is nonsense. This is fiction written by an imposter. In red I write, "Who are you?"

Rain streams down the window. Here is another letter from Cletus Hamburger. It was mailed in Texas. It has a black border, and it reads, "Sorry to hear about Donna. All the more reason for you to join us in El Paso."

Daylight is fading. I open a letter from someone named Angeline. The envelope is scented.

> Dear Dad,
> We are settled at last in a house of our own, with a guest room ready for you whenever you want to use it. I know how lonely you must be, all by yourself.
> Rob has been given a nice raise, but I think he is working too hard. I tell him if he isn't careful, life will pass him by.
> He sends his love.

My strength suddenly drains away. With great effort I brush the perfumed letter off my lap, and it falls to the floor and lies among a scattering of dusty rose petals as the rain, turning to sleet, hits the window with a ping.

Copyright © Jon Hassler. Reprinted from *Redbook*, February 1978.

Jon Hassler was born in Minneapolis and began writing at thirty-seven. After a few years — and eighty-five rejection slips — he began to produce readable fiction, most of it set in fictional Minnesota towns resembling those he lived in. After attending St. John's University, he taught English in high schools, then colleges. His publications include *Staggerford* (1977), *Simon's Night* (1979), *The Love Hunter* (1981) and *A Green Journey* (1985). He is the writer-in-residence at St. John's and won the 1980 Guggenheim Fellowship. His seventh novel, *Grand Opening*, will be published in the winter of 1986.

AUTUMN

Margaret Hasse

THE TREE WHICH IS ALWAYS PRESENT

To praise is the whole thing! A man who can praise
comes toward us like ore out of the silences
of rock. His heart, that dies, presses out
for others a wine that is fresh forever.
— Rainer Maria Rilke, *sonnets to Orpheus*

Raking leaves into piles so her children can jump in
she has forgotten they consider themselves too old
to act like puppies rumpling the heaps.
So the hot little fans she's placed together stay together
in a neatness she doesn't always abide.
The tree she adores. It shakes itself
and drops what isn't essential.
The tree is a tall tree; there're plenty of leaves.
The tree doesn't ask for much, produces these leaves each year.
What the sky gives in sun and water is enough.
Not like the greedy bushes, wilting dramatically
when the gardener is careless or carefree for two days.
Not like the lawn with its need for endless
preening and clipping, seeding and special watering care,
its need for people to stay off with respect,
its need for her on her hands and knees removing dandelions.
The tree is what describes her house:
"Second from the corner, one tree out front . . ."
So she leans on her rake in the crisp applause of late fall,
thanking the tree, its simple cadence of bare branch.
Then thinks of summer when the tree's a single umbrella of shade
allowing her friends to sit like secrets on the porch,
saying how anything is possible, and it's true.

NORTHERN LIGHTS. DULUTH

On the finger of land
beyond the hours
when humans are allowed,
we stop the car,
listen how the breakers
try to beat their way
out of the harbor.
Never has there been
such loud water,
all sound, no sight.
Finally, a smudge
of grey on black
with small blue lights —
a ship.

Arching back, we see
the skies begin
a pulse of red.
These are signs
of an enormous order.
We make vows of silence
and break them
immediately
to talk for hours
about the primitive,
how we saw inside
the body of the sky.

A NOTCH IN THE SPIRAL

We've returned to autumn
Leaving summer a clear lake on which lilies float.
We are back from the season of light,
of lying in warm grass and watching clouds fly;
we're back from a time of round birds,
flagrantly yellow.

Summer still remains in my hair.
Hands sometimes hold sleek water.
There is the sweet cider of apples in store
and two combs of honey on the shelf.

Now the apples on the tree are faces,
the porch light is out,
and we huddle behind our separate doors.

We come back to autumn,
to zucchini that wilt like witches' shoes,
to games of solitaire at night,
to silence in the wake of snow geese
which pass high overhead
and empty our mouths with their cries.

                    — *after a theme of Seferis*

Reprinted with permission of the author from *Stars Above, Stars Below.* (New Rivers Press, St. Paul, Copyright © 1984)

Margaret Hasse began writing poems and diaries when very young, partly in imitation of her mother. After graduating from Stanford University, traveling in Europe and Korea, she moved back to the Midwest and makes her home in Minneapolis where she is the current executive director of Minnesota Alliance for Arts in Education. She has collaborated on two theatrical productions: *Sign of a Child,* 1982, and *Secret Traffic: Four Poets in Performance.* Her first poetry collection, *Stars Above, Stars Below,* was published by the Minnesota Voices Project in 1984.

John Solensten

THE HERON DANCER: A VIGNETTE

"Can you see Dad out there anyplace?" Kristen Hage Ruud asked her husband when he came into the farmhouse kitchen from the grove where he had parked the big tractor under the trees.

"No," he said. He was numb and sullen from sitting for hours over the howl of the tractor engine and his neck was stiff from turning again and again to adjust the four-bottom plow as it turned black-shine furrows in the stubble field. He gave her his "not-now" look, hung his cap on the back of a kitchen chair and began to scrub his hands with a little brush and a thick bar of gray soap.

She moved cheerfully behind him, not saying anything. She knew that if she waited just a little while until he had washed and cooled his face, the heavy tight lines of fatigue around his eyes would smooth out and he would sit and listen and talk to her. But first he had to fret and worry at the mirror, to touch the matted thin hair high on the white forehead protected from the sun. Then he would be looking at her in the mirror and softening from the hard work to a gentleness he always had for her.

The supper was on. "I've eaten, but I'll sit," she said. He sat down heavily, nodded a quick grace, and began to eat very slowly.

"I didn't look for him, but he didn't come out to where I was plowing," he said to Kristen.

"He doesn't like to," she said, sipping some of his coffee to see if it was hot. "He didn't want to make you think he was checking up on you."

"He and I don't see eye-to-eye on plowing."

"He wants to leave grass and bush along the fences," she acknowledged.

"Sure, and that takes acreage away and I have to spray weeds by hand, or you do. And it's bad stuff to handle."

"But he didn't say anything again."

"No, but he can get that look. Only takes him a second to give it to me. But I guess it's all right. It's still his farm. If all I get is a look once in awhile it's not much."

She sipped some more of his coffee. She knew he loved to have her do it. "You want to do something tonight?" he asked her.

"Sure," she said, "but first let's go to the Colony Club for a cocktail. It's cool and nice in there."

He laughed and loved her with his eyes as deeply as he could and she looked at him and smiled.

Kristen was willowy slender in the white summer dress with the navy blue sleeveless blouse. When he stood up she was nearly as tall as he — especially since he had his shoes off. "I'm nearly as tall as you," she said, laughing, ". . . but I've got my summer heels on."

"Well, then, take them off. Come upstairs while I shower and we can dress together and you won't be so tall." His gray eyes were a little serious with desire. He was strong and solid and urgent too. She pushed him away — abruptly, with both hands. "Well," he said, "so that's it? You stiff-arm your man. You got to be courted first tonight I see. Well, well."

She moved in close and touched his face. "You have such a nice mouth," she said. "Did I tell you one of the first things I noticed was your nice mouth?"

"And what about the rest of me?"

"Oh, that was a big bonus — a nice bonus."

"Are you sure you wouldn't..." he began.

"Oh I would, but I'd love to go into town, except that Dad didn't eat anything tonight."

"Oh?"

"He took a sandwich and the old bike and went out by the ditch."

"He'll be all right. He needs to get away from us too. After all, he has to lie downstairs and hear a lot of things. His beautiful daughter upstairs in bed et cetera."

"Oh, well, he doesn't hear. He learned from mother to tune out what he doesn't want to hear, and *I* heard some things too."

He smiled again. "I'll shower and put on the new seersucker slacks and a knit shirt..."

"And the belt I got you — the blue one."

Kristen could see the cottonwoods and elms in the grove as she stood at the window. The leaves of the cottonwoods flashed a dull silver-green in the evening wind. She pursed her lips in worry.

"Could he have had a little stroke or something?" she asked. "He does act strange."

"No, I don't think so. He's got things on his mind. They made a terrible mistake with the ditch. The lake will probably dry up."

"You're almost glad, aren't you?" She turned from the window to say it.

"Do you mean I'm glad we could have maybe 30 more acres of land for crops? It might make all the difference in the world in paying our bills out there. I still owe $9600 on that tractor. But if you mean, do I enjoy seeing the lake we used to canoe on and things just dry up why you know better."

"That was mean. Maybe I get too tall sometimes," she said as he went up the stairs to shower and dress. But still, as she sat at the kitchen table doing her nails she couldn't see the lake through the heavy trees of the grove. Mourning doves fluttered and perched on high dead limbs of the cottonwoods and their coo-i-coo-coo-coo was plaintive and slow. She got up and turned the radio on and finished her nails.

When they were ready to go she asked him if he would drive around the farm to see if they could see her father. "No, honey," he said. "He's all right. He is doing what he wants to do and we should leave him be."

"I suppose people think he's harmless enough," she said as they drove toward Finnmark, the county seat town ten miles north of the farm.

"Oh, he's not harmless," he said, "but he sure isn't helpless either."

"Oh, now you'll make me worry," she said. As she turned to look back, the farm receded into a dim and narrowing dusty corridor between the trees and fields.

"He's all right," he said. "I hope I'm as all right as he is when I get to be 70."

"But he seems so far away," Kristen said, sitting over closer to him.

"You see it?" Nels Hage asked. From where he stood on the west side of Lake Linden he couldn't see the farm buildings where he and his daughter and son-in-law lived, but he was close to the big new drainage ditch. Weeds and grass had not yet grown over the yellow clay banks left by the diggers. From where he stood by his bicycle he could see the ditch cut through the September corn and rivelets of plowing to a distant point where it slanted off toward the Watonwan River. To him the ditch was a great raw wound on the land and on the wide inner landscape of the place he kept in his memory.

"Sure you do," he said. He looked back toward the grass and water reaches of the lake. He squinted and looked to the left and right of the flashing sun path on the water. He was what people in Finnmark called a Black Norwegian. His face was so dark it seemed to be walnut stained. He was gaunt-tall and he had a great beak of a nose. He sniffed the bittersweet algae breath of the water and looked for the heron.

He was there in the shallow water, his legs and plumage phantom silver-blue. "The sky is in your plumes," Hage called to him as if he were listening, "and the God sky is in your eyes and beak." The heron. Stood. Speared deftly and took the fish. Flashed his wings to balance himself.

Hage turned to see the man leaning out of the cab of the green pickup truck. "Jee-pers!" the man laughed. "Did you hear me drive up? Could've run right over you like nothing!" The man dismounted with a clattery, rubbery flap. He wore waders and a yellow raincoat. His face was flushed and thick, his mouth wide and thin like a frog's.

"Could see you a mile away," Hage said. "And heard that damn truck in the bones of my feet. The horn you can shove in your ear. Try to scare every damn thing, don't you?"

"I'm Ransom," the man said.

"I know who you are. What took so long? I sent that Swede governor a letter two months ago. I thought he ate it."

"We just got a letter from the Environmental Protection people two days ago."

"Sure. Took you two days to drive ten miles from town."

"What's this business about our ruining this lake? You said 'killing' in your letter. We don't like being called killers. You come on a little strong."

"Skip all that stuff and take a look for yourself," Hage said. He began to walk down toward the edge of the water. In the light breeze off the lake his blue overalls flapped in the wind and the boniness of him showed — the long bones of his legs strung with old sinews. Ransom clumped angrily after him, his face filled out tightly with anger.

Hage bent over; touched a line of washed-up shells and reed sections. He walked out a little further and knelt down again. "See this?" he said, rooting into another small levee of reeds and sticks and shells.

"It's seasonal," Ransom said, standing over him.

Hage stood up and swung a knotted fist toward the ditch. "It's the ditch, by God!" he cried. "You people put that damn thing so close it's draining the lake and the big farmers know it and wanted it. A lake or a slough is a waste to them. They drive by and say 'we got to get rid of it; it's a hundred acres of corn wasted.'"

"Hell, I'm not standing here all day arguing with you," Ransom said. "We can't turn it back. They won't stand for it."

Ransom was following the old man and puffing. They were at the pickup again and Ransom was on the CB radio in the cab. As he looked out through the windshield he saw Hage pick up the bike and begin to walk it along the ditch. There was a short spade tied crossways behind the seat. Ransom pushed open the door of the pickup and yelled at the old man. "Hold it! Hold it!" And then, talking to someone on the radio mike he said, "See-nile old bird, damn him!" The radio squawked back: "You did the percolation tests, not me!" it said, squawking. "Oh, get off my ass!" Ransom said, and hung up the mike.

Outside, he caught up with Hage. He had to run to do it and he was puffing. It was cooling down on the land around him, the sun giving a final burst of red across the western sky. The birches on the slopes around the lake were white lines slashing across the shadows.

"What's the spade for?" Ransom asked.

"Worms for fishing," Hage said. He held the bike handlebars in his big hands and pushed the bike along like he was guiding a plow.

"Where the hell you going anyway?" Ransom asked.

"I'm going to see him if you don't scare him away."

"Who are you going to see?"

"Him out there, the heron. I shot at him once when I was a kid and my father whipped me for it. He's to be left alone, by God!" Hage was standing tall then. The bike fell over into the grass. He loomed over Ransom like he might pick him up and shake him out of his frog boots.

"Are you all right?" Ransom stared at the old man's face. "It's not the same heron, for God's sake!" he said.

"It's him just the same. Things go on. I'm not my father, but I'm here now. It's not the same water in the lake, but the lake is there. And he — he leaves and comes back every year."

"Not the same," Ransom said. He shook his head sadly. "Tell you what," he said. "Let me put your bike in the back of the pickup and take you back to the house. Your daughter will be worrying about you."

"No, she won't. She don't have to and I'm not crazy either, by God, but I want to know what you're going to do about this ditch of yours."

"It's not *my* ditch. It was put here by all the farmers who voted for it. I'm not even the engineer. I only surveyed it."

"There isn't any way to get at any of you, is there?"

"You knew it was coming."

"Not this close. I told all of you in that meeting in Finnmark that if you got close it would drain the lake."

"What do you expect me to do? Do you expect me to go to them and tell them to move it because Mr. Hage says his heron won't come back?"

"I don't expect anything of you." He picked up the bike again and began pushing it along. "I never did expect anything of you," he said.

"I give up on you." Ransom cried. "And I'll tell you one other thing too. Don't do anything foolish." The old man moved slowly along. "Oh, crap! Now you pretend you can't hear!" At his pickup truck Ransom felt hungry and sweaty and very lonely. He reached for the radio mike and then put it back. He looked out on the water and saw the edge of it receding off the black bottom near the reeds. Down along the edge of the water he saw Nels Hage pushing his bike like a plow, strings of his white hair barely visible. Once he saw Hage turn and look out over the lake and the face was the face of an old prophet — gaunt, fierce and zealous. "Damn old fool!" he muttered as he started the pickup.

Hage saw the wings lift and beat in great uneven pulsings as it lifted off the water. He waited. It sailed up into the purpling dark and then slanted down on pivot wing to land on the western shore near him. After it landed, it began to fish again lifting one foot up gingerly and then pushing it stiffly down. The beak struck. It repeated the movements. The wind brushed Hage's head.

He thought he might walk out there. His legs were stiffening with the night cold, but he thought he might walk out there. It fascinated him, a dance stately and stiff — a dance for an old man, and yet a dance to live, a dance for food, a dance for those who eat and live into the edges of darkness. Yes, a dance for those who wait for the morning.

He thought he might walk there, but he sat down. The sandwich was good — sausage and thick bread. After he had eaten, he folded the lunch sack carefuly and put it into his pocket. Over the nightfall dark an order of stars moved.

He worked slowly and steadily, levering the lumps of clay down into the ditch with the spade. He felt very strong doing it. Above the clay dam the water widened and slowed and deepened. "Yes, by God. You betcha, by God!" he kept saying as he filled in the ditch.

Reprinted from *The Heron Dancer and Other Stories of the North* (New Rivers Press, Copyright © 1981) with the author's permission.

John Solensten teaches literature and writing at Concordia College, St. Paul, Minnesota. His book-length published works include *The Heron Dancer and Other Stories of the North*, 1981, *Good Thunder*, 1983, and *There Lies a Fair Land*, 1985. His plays have been produced at Center Stage, Minneapolis; the Tulsa Center for the Performing Arts; and the Duluth Community Playhouse. He began his writing career while working as a public information writer for IDS in Minneapolis. He defines himself as a "regionalist" with certain "droll" Scandinavian-American propensities.

Marisha Chamberlain

THE STARS ARE APPLE CLUSTERS

Exhaustion builds a maze of branches
behind my eyes the first day
I pick apples. Day's end, my hands

still reach to pick. Like gloves
gone threadbare, gloves with holes
I put those hands away

in my pockets. Darkness unleashes stars
and I connect them in dark trees: the leaping
impulse of my hand toward the studded

branch. A dream smears me apple red
and apple green: I straddle a dozen
gleaming ladders, roll apples

into my mouth to collect in my half-bushel
stomach with the trap door chute
to a crate big as an empty city.

Night falls down on my head like a tarp.
I rip a hole in the night
and reach up to pick the stars.

END OF THE SEASON

Overnight freeze,
the apples
send their spirits
back through the twigs,
the branches,
the trunk of the tree.
They go limp
from inside out.

In the picking
crew's quarters,
the breakfast cook
is up and washing
in cold water.
By the pump, he squints
at the sun
on the apple trees,
the hanged fruit,
the end of the money.

DESIRE FOR COLD

In late afternoon of the year: late fall,
I abandon my peace with the sun, put on
the rough twilight jacket, push
the buttons through slits only by feel
in the dim light, make myself, not cozy but
ready: dress like a soldier,
eager for the future.

Dawn had worn my thin, pink dress. Keep it!
I forswear spring when I dressed
carelessly, not quite naked, but always askew:
a strap always slipping off a shoulder.
I break faith with casual summer,
the need for shelter only at night
to block the stars that distract from sleep,
to keep the dew off.

As cold, at first invisible, puts trees
to the torch, then strips their leaves, as each day,
colder, brings clarity, each day, clearer and
death more active: not summer's lenient decay
but the bite in the air, everywhere — I stretch
my hand through the open door to feel the cold,
approaching night. Nothing clearer than cold
to fight and I need to fight.

MONA LISA

1

The sun sets as I drive down from Red Wing.
I leave behind me, by dark,
the big lake, the sugarloaf,
the white rock where the Indian woman
leaped to her death in the water.
Maiden Rock. As I pass beneath it,
she plunges again into the river,
then out of a watery chrysallis,
her body gathered in a single curve:
the moon rising red behind a skin of cloud.
Swollen at the horizon,
now the moon condenses, whitens,
climbs the sky,
takes its place on top of the dark
below it like a black dress
and out of a black coif it shines,
the craters of the moon
through the gauze of distance:
the features of a face
and a smile.

2

I'm small and home sick.
Mother lays out for me the big black book,
Art Masterpieces, its cover so heavy
I must lift with two hands.
I move through the cave bulls, El Greco's storm,
the journey of the Magi with monkeys,
til I find my woman.

I see nothing remarkable in her smile:
I don't know yet this is the Mona Lisa
and not the mother of God. Her face, more godly
than the frightened virgin, more certain
than Mary at the foot of the cross;
this unknown Italian woman
through da Vinci's hand gathered
all the lost in a curve
before she stood,
stepped away from the painter
into her perishing world.

"The Stars Are Apple Clusters," "Mona Lisa," "End of the Season," "Desire for Cold" from *Powers,* Copyright © 1983, by Marisha Chamberlain, reprinted by permission of New Rivers Press. "The Stars Are Apple Clusters" originally appeared in *Dacotah Territory.* "Mona Lisa" originally appeared in *Great River Review.*

Marisha Chamberlain moved to Minnesota in 1969 to attend Macalester College and has lived here ever since. She was the recipient of grants from the Bush and Loft-McKnight Foundations, and a poetry Fellowship from National Endowment for the Arts Fellowship. *Scheherazade,* a full-length play, won a Dramatists Guild/CBS New Plays Program award in 1984 and was seen on public television. Her stories and poems have appeared in numerous literary magazines and anthologies, including *Dacotah Territory, Great River Review* and *25 Minnesota Writers. Powers,* 1984, is her first book.

Meridel LeSueur

from
THE ANCIENT PEOPLE AND
THE NEWLY COME

There is no place in the world with summer's end, fall harvest, and Indian summer as in Minnesota. They used to have husking bees. The wagons went down the corn rows, and the men with metal knives on their fingers cut the ears off the stalks and tossed them into the wagons. Then they husked the ears, dancing afterward, and if a man got a red ear he could kiss his girl. In August there were great fairs, and the farmers came in to show their crops and beasts, and the workers showed their new reapers and mowers.

There was the excitement of the fall, the terror of the winter coming on. In the winter we didn't have what we did not can, preserve, ferment, or bury in sand. We had to hurry to cut the wood and to get the tomatoes, beans, and piccalilli canned before frost in the garden. It was like preparing for a battle. My grandmother wrapped the apples in newspaper and put them cheek by jowl in the barrels. Cabbage was shredded and barreled for sauerkraut. Even the old hens were killed. I was always surprised to see my gentle grandmother put her foot on the neck of her favorite hen and behead her with a single stroke of a long-handled axe.

The days slowly getting shorter, the herbs hung drying as the woods turned golden. Everything changes on the prairies at the end of summer, all coming to ripeness, and the thunderheads charging in the magnetic moisture of the vast skies. The autumnal dances are the best medicine against the threat of winter, isolation again, dangers. The barns were turned into dance halls before the winter hay was cut. The women raised their long skirts and danced toward hell in schottisches, round dances, and square dances. The rafters rang with the music of the old fiddlers and the harmonica players.

When the golden leaves stacked Persian carpets on the ground and the cornfields were bare, we saw again the great hunched land naked, sometimes fall plowed or planted in winter wheat. Slowly the curve seemed to rise out of the glut of summer, and the earth document was visible script, readable in the human tenderness of risk and ruin.

The owl rides the meadow at his hunting hour. The fox clears out the pheasants and the partridges in the cornfield. Jupiter rests above Antares, and the fall moon hooks itself into the prairie sod. A dark wind flows down from Mandan as the Indians slowly move out of the summer campground to go back to the reservation. Aries, buck of the sky, leaps to the outer rim and mates with earth. Root and seed turn into flesh. We turn back to each other in the dark together, in the short days, in the dangerous cold, on the rim of a perpetual wilderness.

The great richness of growing up in a northwest village was in the variety and the excitement of all the ethnic cultures. I was free to go into all of them, even singing in Norwegian choirs and dancing with Finnish dance groups. The rituals were still celebrated. There was even a bagpipe group that marched on St. Patrick's Day, all in green, and in the park I listened to a lawyer, three sheets in the wind, recite the last speech of Robert Emmet. I liked to sample the rich foods, too, and secretly found in myself a riotous temperament different from my grandmother's.

I especially loved the dances. They were so colorful and varied, and some were so sensual and beautiful. They freed me from severe puritan sexual rigidity, from relating pleasure to guilt and sin. I remember my first dance. I don't know how my mother and my grandmother let me go, but it was not without warnings, threats, and a terrible armor against sin and excess. My first party dress was white, although I would have preferred red or even yellow. But only Polish whores wore those colors, my grandmother said. So I wore a white dress and shoes that had a thin stripe of red around them and little heels. I had rolled my hair on newspaper to have curls, which seemed to me the height of voluptuousness.

Jon came to pick me up in a surrey with a fringe on top, though it was harnessed to a plow horse. The harvest was just over, and his huge forearms were browned from the sun and gleaming.

He smelled of chaff, even though he was scrubbed to within an inch of his life and his wild straw hair was slicked down with bear grease. He seemed strange and huge as helped me onto the high step. We drove slowly through the aspens, which were gold around us. I smelled of talcum powder and so did he. I had rubbed wet crepe paper on my cheeks and blackened my eyes with kitchen matches, passing my grandmother quickly so she couldn't see my whorish color.

The old horse turned, laughing, to see if we were there, we were so silent. In the grove wagons and carriages had stopped for spooning as it was early. I was glad we weren't going to do that. My grandmother had told me to drink nothing, just as Demeter told Persephone not to eat anything in Hades, though of course she did and was trapped by pomegranate seeds. She warned me that even grape punch could easily be tampered with. She meant spiked.

In the big empty hall everyone stood around kidding and waiting. The men seemed very tall and hung their heads. The girls seemed unbearably bright, each in her best bib and tucker, all laughing too loud and embracing each other to show how good it was to embrace.

But soon the bung was pulled from the beer barrel. Mugs were filled, and moonshine was nipped outside the door. But lips that touch liquor shall never touch mine. Besides, I was bold and spiced enough, going out with a boy, wearing almost high heels, and waiting to dance for the first time.

The fiddlers started warming up. An accordion joined them and we were off. I began to be tossed from one tall man to another. My feet hardly touched the ground, and the caller could have been speaking another language. I didn't need to know the dance, I just followed. I went from one great harvester to the other. They were laughing, some yelling and "feeling you up," as the girls said. Through the hours we were flying, sweating, pressed, tossed, stamping out the rhythms, whirling from embrace to embrace, touching — Hitch 'em up and hike 'em up a high tuckahaw, give me the dance of turkey in the straw. Sugar in the gourd, honey in the horn, I never was so happy since the day I was born.

As the night got deeper and the fiddlers hotter, we were flung into the men's arms, back and forth, a weave of human bodies. I couldn't tell one from the other. A girl took me outside with her. The girls lifted their skirts on one side of the field, and the boys stood with their backs to us on the other. I never heard such laughter or sensed such dangerous meaning in the night, in what took place in the woods, when the dancers returned with curious smiles and leaves in their hair. We seemed on the edge of some abysmal fire. But they seemed unafraid, plunging into the heat and the danger as if into a bonfire of roses.

I never was the same again.

University of Minnesota Press, Minneapolis. Copyright © 1976, University of Minnesota. From "The Ancient People and the Newly Come," reprinted from *Growing Up in Minnesota: Ten Writers Remember Their Childhoods* by permission of the University of Minnesota Press.

Meridel LeSueur, born in 1900, has been many things: a student and teacher of dance and theater groups, a Hollywood actress and stunt woman, a lecturer, and a teacher, conducting classes in short story writing. She lives in Minneapolis, Minnesota, with 10 books and over 150 articles to her credit. She attended the University of Wisconsin and the American Academy of Dramatic Art. Her stories have appeared eight times in the O'Brien annual anthology of *Best American Short Stories,* and one story, "Annunciation," has been described as an American masterpiece.

Jeanette Hinds

BACHELOR UNCLE

Barley Field

"He will have you running around until
the day he dies," my father said.
I knew my father spoke from insight branded in
The day he set up barley shocks beneath a liquid sun
    Straw-end down; grain-heads tilted in;
    Eight bundles in a wigwam shape
    With one to cap the top against a rain.

Weed stumps among the rows of stubble
Jabbed beneath his shoes.
Barley beards needled the collar of a shirt
Stuck to his back in one large stain of sweat.

Standing in the evening shadow of the barn,
My uncle paid him.
    Half pay (and done with flourish too)
Because my father was a relative
Expected to help out; to work for less.

My father brought his seeds of anger home
To germinate in long ambivalence.

Transition

The farmhouse sags into a north wind.
Light snow is matted at the roots of grasses,
Scatterings of oak leaves hang like rags
From wrinkled arms of oak. Old rustlings
Churn along the gray November chill:
A fight with knives behind the grocery store,
A homely girl who moped about the house,
A girl in town who washed the dancing shirts,
Town-folk who kept their distance from a man
Who always "took the big end of the stick,"
Two quiet sisters who merely walked away...

But time and decay converge on man and farm.
My uncle is alone in the backwaters of his need;
Aground on rocks of his self-choosing.
And I, bearing barley needles in my mind,
    Have come.

Autumn Departure

I help you to the edge of the bed.
Your catheter came out last night;
It is a gummy worm on the linoleum.
I dress you in my father's underwear
(Summer shorts; only pair around.)
Your arms are stiff wings difficult to fold
Into the sleeves of a red flannel shirt.
I guide your feet into shoes; stand you up;
Zipper the trousers; tighten the belt.

In the car, you wear a new cap
With the bill pulled into a straight line.
You guess the moisture content in the corn
Hinged and hung along the brittle fields.
I watch your mind clutch the common world
To slow the hours.
    But life and road must end
Where black poles calibrate the miles to overtake
Eternity across the county line.

Waiting Rooms

"He will have you running around until
the day he dies," my father had said.
I study the waiting room floor:
    Two black, one white, three gray —
    I remember other squares of time.

One night you almost died. I hovered
Like a limp bird, fluttering your hand away
When you plucked the intravenous needle.
Your eyes swam into bloodshot consciousness,
Checking whether I was there —
A face to mark you through disoriented worlds.

I brought you home with an indwelling catheter.
The plastic tube shoved into your body
    was painful to see —
Like a kingbird choke-swallowing a fish.
I took your boxes to the laundromat —
Overalls stiff with drooled food,
Towels beyond bleaching.
    My hands recoiled.
Your teeth soaked in a cracked cup.
Food floated along the brim.
    My hands recoiled.

What purpose do you serve?
What purpose do I serve?
    You are hooks pressed into me;
    Your eyes catch at me
    Like blue shards.

Hospital Lights

You lie on a narrow cart waiting for
The fingers of medicine to analyze you.
The nurse is aloof. You are a bit of flotsam
Drifted in to smudge her sterile sheets.
Though this is so, her face will never tell
For she has learned the stiff civility
Drawn on each morning with her starched cap.

Your bony hand circles the side rails,
Your fingers tighten down with pain.
(The nails need clipping.) They are claws
Tightening around a willow branch in dusky rain.

   You have become an object,
   A two-dimensional shape,
   A shade on a white sheet in a white room.

   My mind touches cold perimeters,
   A limit where I cannot comprehend
      Your suffering.

The stiff-capped nurse wheels you through
   The double-doors
      Of health and sickness;
      Of love and contempt;
      Of life and death.

Answered Need

Your head is a small shell,
The skin stretched along the cheeks
Conforms to a skull now surfacing.

What seed of sleep can mind fold in upon
When wings of death beat against the dark?
What warping and what straightening is here?
What end to greed and all self-centering?

I try to think of nights when you went dancing
Sending all the females in the house
Into a flurry of errands — like brown birds
Bringing bits of straw and string in their beaks.

I try to see you as you shall emerge at last,
    Clean-shaven; spit-shined;
        Wearing a silk shirt.
But outer dance has ended in this inner time.

Old barley needles linger in my mind,
For I have "run around" until this day.
Yet now, I judge not — judging makes me blind —
I had my bushels under which I hid
My flickering love — wavering when I knew
You were the cup that could not pass from me;
You were my work on earth to do.

    How late I learn
    Love asks nothing in return.

Jeanette Hinds, a longtime resident of Rochester, Minnesota, has been a high school teacher, an editorial assistant in the Mayo Clinic Section of Publications, and an assistant librarian. Born in Ellendale, Minnesota, she received her B.S. at Mankato State University and her M.A. at the University of Wisconsin. She is a member of the Root River Poets, and managing co-editor of *Streets & Towers,* their annual poetry magazine. Over fifty of her poems have been published, many in *McCall's, Farm Journal, Christian Century,* as well as literary magazines.

WINTER

Carol Bly

GREAT SNOWS

> *How strange to think of giving up all ambition!*
> *Suddenly I see with such clear eyes*
> *The white flake of snow*
> *That has just fallen in the horse's mane.*
> — "Watering the Horse," by Robert Bly,
> *Silence in the Snowy Fields*

It is sometimes mistakenly thought by city people that grownups don't love snow. They think only children who haven't got to shovel it love snow, or only people like the von Fürstenburgs and their friends who get to go skiing in exotic places and will never backslope a roadside in all their lives: that is a mistake. The fact is that most country or small-town Minnesotans love snow. They relish snow in large inconvenient storms; they like the excesses of it, they like the threat of it, the endless work of it, the glamour of it.

Before a storm, Madison is full of people excitedly laying in food stocks for the three-day blow. People lay in rather celebratory food, too. Organic-food parents get chocolate for the children; weight watchers lay in macaroni and Sara Lee cakes; recently-converted vegetarians backslide to T-bones. People hang around the large SuperValu window and keep a tough squinty-eyed watch on the storm progress with a lot of gruff, sensible observations (just like Houston Control talking to the moon, very much on top of it all) like "Ja, we need this for spring moisture..." or "Ja, it doesn't look like letting up at all..." or "Ja, you can see where it's beginning to drift up behind the VFW." The plain pleasure of it is scarcely hidden.

That is before the storm. Then the town empties out as the farmers and their families take their stocks home before U.S. 75, Minnesota 40, and Lac Qui Parle 19 close up. During the storm itself heroism is the routine attitude. I remember once when the phone was out, before all the telephone lines went underground, and the power was off, our neighbor came lightly in his huge pack boots across the drift top, high up from our house level, like an upright black ant, delicately choosing his footing over the hard-slung and paralyzed snow waves. He looked as if he were walking across a frozen North Atlantic. He had come over to see if we were O.K. It was before snowmobiles, at –40 degrees a welcome gesture.

Then right after a storm we all go back uptown because we have to see how the town has filled. The streets are walled ten and eleven feet high. If they had had underground parking ramps in the pyramids this is what they'd have looked like, white-painted, and we crawl between the neatly carved clean walls. The horrible snow buildup is a point of pride. In 1969 a fine thing happened: the county of Lac Qui Parle imported a couple of gigantic snow-removal machines from Yellowstone Park. It cost several thousand dollars to get those monsters here; when they arrived our heavy, many-layered, crusted snow broke the machines — they couldn't handle it. With glittering eyes we sent them back to Yellowstone Park.

Snowdrifts in the bad years, as in 1969, force us to dump garbage and nonburnables ever nearer the house, until finally in March there is a semicircle of refuse nearly at the front door. Even the German shepherd lowers his standards; the snow around the doghouse entrance is unspeakable.

If one has any kind of luck one garners comfort from great weather, but if there is some anxious and unresolved part of one's inner life, snowfall and certainly snowboundness can make it worse. During the winter of 1968-69, the three doctors of our town prescribed between two and three times as much tranquilizing medicine as usual. And Robert Frost, despite being one of the best snow poets going, has an odd, recurring fretfulness about snow:

> The woods are lovely, dark and deep,
> But I have promises to keep

What promises? To whom? If we think about it it sounds moralistic and self-denying — a moral showing-off in some way. The nervousness is stronger, though, in "Desert Places":

> Snow falling and night falling fast, oh, fast
> In a field I looked into going past,
> And the ground almost covered smooth in snow,
> But a few weeds and stubble showing last.
>
> The woods around it have it — it is theirs.
> All animals are smothered in their lairs.
> I am too absent-spirited to count;
> The loneliness includes me unawares.

I am struck by the malaise of the word *absent-spirited*. It must mean — this joy in snow or fretfulness in snow — that whatever is providential and coming to each of us from within is sped the faster by snowfall.

Being out in a blizzard is not lovely. Nature then feels worse than inimical; it feels simply impersonal. It isn't that, like some goddess in Homer, she wants to grab and freeze your body in her drifts; it is that you can be taken and still the wind will keep up its regular blizzard whine and nothing has made a difference. In February of 1969 the fuel men couldn't get through for weeks; one midnight my husband and I had to transfer oil from a drum behind an old shed to our house tank. We did this in cans, load after load, crawling on all fours and rolling in the ravines between the drifts. It had some nice moments: every ten minutes or so we'd meet behind the old shed, when one returned an empty can and the other was coming away with a full one, and we'd crouch in the scoured place, leaning over the nasty, rusted, infuriatingly slow spigot of the oil tank there. Looking at each other, we saw we had that impersonal aspect of snow-covered people. It was peculiar to think that anyone behind those freezing, melting, refreezing eyebrows ever objected to an act of Congress or ever loved a summer woods or memorized the tenor to anything by Christopher Tye. Back inside, our job done, still cold and rough-spoken, still walking like bears, we studied the children in their beds.

To us in Minnesota a blizzard in itself is of no practical good, but it is interesting how useful blizzards can be. Ordinary snowfall, not moved into deep-packed areas by wind, runs off too quickly in the spring and can't be controlled for good use. *The Proceedings of the American Society of Civil Engineers* has essay after essay on uses of Rocky Mountain snowmelt. Twenty-five hundred years ago, and possibly even earlier, the Persians used deep-drifted snow for irrigation. They built their *quanats*. Quanats are brick-walled tunnels running from the snowfields of the Elburz and other mountain ranges of Iran to villages fifteen or twenty miles away. At a point in the mountains' water table still higher than the land level of the parched miles and miles to be irrigated, the arched brick tunnels were carefully sloped to keep the water moving. The "mother well" was 200 feet deep and deeper. These 22,000 tunnels (there were 30,000 in 1960 but 8,000 were not in working condition) had airshafts for fresh air and maintenance access every 50 to 60 yards. Darius took the qanat technique to Egypt in the 5th century B.C. Nothing could have been cultivated in three-fourths of the now-irrigated fields of Iran without the ancient qanats. Persia was the originator of melons, cucumbers, and pears.

This is just to give an idea of mankind's long use of heavily drifted snow. Since we don't *use* blizzards in western Minnesota, the question lingers: why the pleasure in great weather? As with children in thunderstorms, I think we all have a secret affair of long standing with the other face of things. Children want the parents and the police and the other irritating powers to have their measure taken; they want a change of justice; but it goes further: they have a secret affection for bad weather.

Storms, what is more, force us to look at nature closely, and that is never boring. All meetings of the Business Improvement Association and the Countryside Council and the play rehearsal committees stop in a blizzard. It is a help. Two things make nature lovely to people, I think: enforced, extended leisure in a natural place — which storms give us out here; and second, planning our own lives instead of just following along. The moment, for example, that someone finally decides not to take the promising job offered by Reserve Mining, for example, or the moment someone decides not to pad a travel-expense account at the Ramada is a moment in which ice and snow and bare trunks look better, less happenstance, less pointless. C. S. Lewis goes very far: he claims that the fact that we all agree on what is meant by *good* or *holy* (that is, no one thinks robbery or despoiling the land or depriving the poor is good) indicates that goodness and holiness are actually a normal, planned part of our universe — perfectly natural to the species. He would not be surprised at all to see snow on a horse's mane all the better for having just worked out an ethical decision.

"Great Snows" from *Letters From the Country* by Carol Bly. Copyright © 1981 by Carol Bly. Reprinted by permission of Harper & Row, Publishers, Inc.

Carol Bly, who lives in Madison, Minnesota, is the author of *Letters From the Country,* 1981, as well as *Backbone,* 1985, her collection of short stories, and *Soil and Stewardship,* 1986. Her work has appeared in *The New Yorker* and *American Review,* and "The Quality of Life" was included in *The Best American Short Stories of 1983.* A recipient of grants from the Minnesota State Arts Board and the Bush Foundation, she lectures and teaches writing, and tells her students "Learning without reflection is meaningless; reflection without learning is dangerous."

Kevin FitzPatrick

SPLIT HOCKEY STICK

It is almost dark. He can no longer see his running
friends, though he hears their laughter-like screams
far up the alley. Above his head his red stocking-cap
is glowing fainter. It is a last ember in an apple
tree that has been charred by winter.

He can't go home without it. But they threw it there —
still she would send him right back before he could
take off an overshoe. It would be darker. But he
has tried almost everything: jumping and climbing,
shaking the tree and snowballs. If he was only taller —
still he is too tall to count on tears and too
tall to count on a giant who would stop and from way
on the sidewalk swat it to him with a huge mittened
hand.

He will be happy for anyone walking slowly home through
snow in the dark, anyone a couple inches taller, who
would put a lunch bucket or shopping bag down to help
him. Until then he will continue, though his face is
getting redder, trying, though it hurts his toes, to
kick loose a split hockey stick that is long enough —
but seems stuck to the earth with cement.

MITTENS

When winter shivers me
like a swimmer dipping
into an icy pool
and though I'm wearing gloves
each finger stiffens
like a body in a long drawer
I switch to mittens
sheltering my fingers
like snowed-in friends
who thaw
accept their close lodging
and now and then
perform short skits
until the weather warms.

"Mittens" previously appeared in the *Sackbut Review,* Vol. 1, #2, Copyright © 1979 Kevin FitzPatrick. Reprinted by permission of the author.

Kevin FitzPatrick has published poems in *Lactuca, Light Year '86,* and *Sanctuary, Si!* He is the editor of the *Lake Street Review* in Minneapolis where he lives, having grown up in St. Paul across the Lake Street bridge. For the past five years, he has worked in downtown St. Paul as a claims examiner for the State of Minnesota. He draws his inspiration for poems usually from urban themes, people and settings.

Laurel Winter

MIGRATING

Edith never knew when there might be birds perched near the window. If she moved stiffly, favoring her arthritic knee, the birds took flight. So, at seventy-seven, she learned to walk as if she were a woman of her grandmother's generation, smooth and stately in a hoop skirt. Her younger sister — noting the graceful movements on one of her frequent, almost parental visits — asked if she had been waltzing to the music of the old Victrola.

"No," Edith said, with a wisp of smile just below the surface. "Actually, I've been studying bird etiquette." Margaret Ann had given her such a searching look that she regretted the small, private joke.

But Margaret Ann drove off in her blue Ford and there were only the birds: pert brown-gray hoppers, stem-legged runners with white cravats, the smooth-diving swallows. She regretted that she knew they were swallows — she would have called them something entirely different — but it was inescapable common knowledge and she bore the burden of it without more than an occasional sigh. It could have been worse; she might have been positive that the brown-gray hoppers were sparrows.

As it was, she enjoyed them without classifying them and burned the ornithology book from the dark walnut bookshelf in the fireplace. The pages curled into ash, unread, as Edith warmed herself at the flames.

More and more of the birds seemed to congregate around the stone bungalow that their grandmother had left to her. Edith had lived in the bungalow since she was seventeen and Margaret Ann was an infant. Their mother had died from giving birth and their father, soon after, from giving up. It was the only place that seemed like home to her. Her sister had never learned to love it, even though it was the only home she knew as a child.

Edith took care of her grandmother during the long period when she was aged and incontinent until the old woman's death almost forty years ago. Forty years of peace. Now, Margaret Ann was trying to take care of her.

She sighed and wandered through the rooms, touching the marble vanity, the warped sash of the dormer window, the flocked parlor wallpaper. "Do I need taking care of?" Her wavery reflection in the hallway mirror didn't answer. She realized that she had not combed her hair, maybe for several days, and sighed again.

It was easier to think about the birds. She couldn't ever remember such a profusion of them and — with a modest conceit — felt that there was more attraction than the chunks of wire-clad suet, the decanters of hummingbird ale, the receptacles of tan-burnished seed. "We are more than casual acquaintances," she said, settling into the brocade windowseat, "more like formal friends."

And like friends one has spent much time with, she knew what she would see when she looked out the window: the red bird cracking sunflower seeds in its chunky beak, or the brown-gray hoppers ignoring her, fighting for the best of the eight perches on the nearest feeder.

"Delightful," she said, as if they had asked after her health. It was easy to lie, remembering the quavering complaints of her grandmother. "Just delightful. And you?"

It was snowing when she first ventured out onto the porch, carrying a rocking chair with difficulty, then — after her wheezing had abated — returning with an moss-green afghan and a rug for her knees. The birds had flown, of course, with the unusual opening of the heavy front door, but she was very still, keeping the chair from rocking, and soon they returned.

As was her habit, she spoke to them, "Yes, it is a little brisk." The birds — usually shielded from her voice by the diamond panes of leaded glass — exploded into flight at the sound, causing her to rock backwards and clutch the afghan to her neck. By the time her palpitations had lessened, and her ankles chilled where the rug didn't reach, the birds were back again.

It was a bad season to begin a personal relationship, but she had begun, so she didn't waver. She carried the chair out each morning, wearing her navy coat and two pair of hose, as well as her galoshes. The wind flirted leaves around her feet but she endured the cold, huddled into the afghan and a quilt that her grandmother had made.

Often she feared — and half-hoped — that the birds would be migrating soon, because of the way their feathers ruffled, puffed against the gusts. The suet went fast now, and so did the seeds. Every crisp morning she had to refill the containers, the air biting her lungs and condensing in white puffs as she exhaled, her footing hesitant on the slick snow.

The boy who delivered the groceries offered to fill the feeders for her once, but she declined. "Thank you all the same," she said, writing out the check for his service. It amazed her how angry — or perhaps jealous — the offer made her. She had to tear up the check and write another, because she'd signed in the wrong place. "Thank you," she repeated, more abruptly. The boy went away shaking his head, his coat halfway unzipped as if the weather had no affect on him.

But it was cold. The brown-gray hoppers were gone one day in December. They were small, she reasoned. Better that they had gone or they would have frozen. For almost an hour, she speculated on the places they could have gone: Madeira, the Canary Islands, Ecuador. Lovely warm places. Was Madeira warm?

She tasted the word on her tongue. "Madeira." Was it even a place? She preferred to think that it was — a warm place — and that the small birds had flown safely there. She thought about them, hopping on coral rocks in the sunshine, until the wind invaded the edge of the quilt and burrowed through the afghan. Then she went in, carrying the chair with her.

If she had just continued to take the chair in, she decided later, everything would have been all right. But it was oak, and heavy. She began leaving it out on the porch, sweeping the accumulated snow off with a whiskbroom before she sat down.

The chair was out, with just a skiff of snow on the arms and seat when her sister arrived with Christmas packages. Edith tried to keep her in the stone-flagged kitchen with a cup of tea, but Margaret Ann would have none of that, preferring to inspect the entire bungalow. Had it been a little darker, she may not have noticed, or if the red bird hadn't suddenly alighted on the chair arm, as it had begun to do, even when Edith was sitting in it.

At any rate, her sister saw, and was not put off by the weak excuse that it had broken and been set out of the way. The drifting snow had not obliterated the frequent tracks, and the afghan, quilt, and whiskbroom were lying together in a neat pile by the front door. It was all too incriminating, and Edith sighed.

"I've become something of a birdwatcher," she admitted, hoping to get off with that.

Margaret Ann sniffed. "Outside?"

"Only when it's nice out."

"You're not well as it is." She held her palm against Edith's forehead and frowned.

Edith winced at the chill of her sister's hand. "I'm fine," she said, lifting her shoulders and smiling. "Really."

It did not end there. Margaret Ann drove her into Bemidji for a physical, and pursed her lips when Edith admitted to having a cough sometimes. It wasn't much of a cough, she told the doctor, hunching her wrinkled skin away from the icy stethoscope. Hardly anything at all.

Apparently he disagreed. "Is there a possibility she could move in with you?" he asked Margaret Ann, speaking as if Edith weren't there, as if she were a child.

"No." Edith spoke firmly. "I have lived alone too long to want a roommate now." The statement was only partly successful.

Margaret Ann, her forehead encased in worry lines, made a series of arrangements quickly — rather like one of the white-cravat runners, darting from problem to problem as if they were clumps of dry grass to explore. Edith knew the futility of protest, as Margaret Ann had inherited the full measure of her grandmother's nature, and it was arranged all too soon; the deliveries stopped, the bungalow rented to a young couple with children, a nice apartment leased in Bemidji.

On one point Edith was adamant: the birds must be fed. It was a commitment, she explained to her sister; when one started feeding them, they expected it to continue and they stayed around rather than migrating. Then, if one forgot, they starved and froze to death. It was an obligation.

Finally, Margaret Ann relented and arranged with the grocery-delivery boy to fill the feeders. She probably told him to fill only one feeder, Edith thought, looking out the small apartment window at the brick building next door, just to keep to the letter of the promise. She could never confirm it though, because her sister became very busy and would not take her out to the bungalow. Not even to just drive by, although she wasn't too busy to check on Edith almost every day.

Edith missed the dark wainscoting of the bungalow, the fireplace made of river stones set in gray mortar, the surrounding grove of tamaracks and red cedar. She had lived there, in the forest, for sixty years. The apartment seemed too modern, even though it was at least fifteen years old; the bungalow had stood since her grandparents settled near the town of Cass Lake in 1884. What little furniture she'd been able to bring did not rest well between the slick white walls.

She hadn't bothered to bring the Christmas tree Margaret Ann had provided for her. Strung with popcorn and cranberry chains, she had left it on the porch for the birds. Now, there was no convenient porch for the rocker, where she could sit, hoping her birds would find her.

Just in case they did, she took to crumbling her bread and leaving it on the outside of the window sill, even though the window was hard to open. There were no trees nearby to break the wind, so the crumbs generally blew off, into the snow, but a bird did finally come, perching on the narrow ledge, toes flat and awkward against the aluminum.

Its feathers were shiny black, with purple-green undertones, and it was not shy. When there was no bread waiting, it would open its beak and emit a raucous caw directly at the window. Edith always hurried then, sometimes grating a little cheese if she had no bread, jerking the window open. The bird would fly a short distance and return the second that the window closed. It went on like that for almost a month, until late in January, when she decided to leave the window open. She hooked the chain into the slot at the door, so Margaret Ann couldn't catch her.

With the heat on high and her chenille robe over her clothes, it wasn't too cold. "Not cold at all," she said to the bird, hoping her shivers would not frighten it. At the sound of her voice, it flew away. "Come back." She leaned as far as she dared out the window, hoping to see the bird. "Please, come back. You shouldn't be afraid of me."

She was hunched in a kitchen chair when the bird returned, cawing for its food. "You came," she whispered. "I didn't think you would."

It was not long before the bird was used to her voice, and she kept up a patter of endless talk, things she wanted to say and hadn't said yet. "Margaret Ann should have married," she told the bird. "It would have been better for her." And for me, she thought, but she didn't say that, not yet.

"Madeira. I wonder how the hoppers are doing in Madeira. Soon they will fly back and fight at the feeder that the grocery-delivery boy fills." She fell silent, wondering if the bungalow's renters had taken down even that one feeder, wondering if they had a stalking cat? A Siamese perhaps? "Stay in Madeira," she whispered, stroking the white wall, wishing it were the wood around the old attic dormer.

"Sometimes I don't feel old at all." The bird preened its breast feathers. "And then I see my hand, just like my grandmother's hand before she died. I hope you never have to go through that, get all withered up. Would you still be able to fly?"

After one of Margaret Ann's visits, Edith crumbled the coffee cake her sister had brought. "I wish she would let me go home." Her hands clenched, rendering the cake she held into a dense ball. She dropped it on the floor, turning to the window where the bird was squawking at her. "But you don't know where I used to live, do you?" For a moment, she tried to formulate some way of directing the black bird to the bungalow, then she shook her head and tossed the pile of sweet crumbs out the window. Most of them fell into the snow below.

"Do come in," she told the bird, peering at her through the black beads of its eyes. When it didn't enter, she shrugged and shook her head. "Very well."

When Margaret Ann knocked on the door, she would flick the crumbs from the sill, close the window, and hang her robe in the closet — all without abruptness. I was resting, she would say, when queried about her slowness. She tried not to cough at all, or even clear her throat. Margaret Ann would inspect and depart, never truly satisfied, it seemed.

"I do believe she's waiting to find me with a broken hip, or wandering around the living room, nude and senile. Just because she's seventeen years younger...."

It was almost the middle of February, and the breeze was still wintery, but she knew the tamarack trees around the bungalow would be showing fresh green soon, and birds would begin nesting. "You won't leave, will you?" she asked the bird, heaping the sill with bread. The bird cocked its head at her and pecked the pile of crumbs. "Did you hear me?" she asked. "I want you to stay with me."

When that bread was gone, Edith pushed the table over to the window, leaning against it twice to rest and shiver. She tore a bun into small pieces and placed them, not on the sill, but in a trail across the table, the first bit just inside the window. The bird was tentative, snatching one chunk and flying away for almost an hour. She sat in a chair and shivered, not bothering to close the open neck of her robe.

"Come back...come back...come...." Her soft whisper became a litany.

Until the bird returned.

She had to get the bird to a spot just past the middle of the table, she decided, if she was to have time to close the window before it could fly out. One crumb after another, she lured it in.

When it was at the spot and a little beyond, she reached past it, smoothly, and pulled down on the window as hard as she could. It caught, and she had to tug.

The bird snapped into flight, as if it had never been anything but wild, and careened around the room for a brief instant before aiming directly at the clear, closed pane of glass. Edith screamed — stuffing the lapel of her robe into her mouth to stifle the sound — when it hit the window and dropped to the crumb-littered table.

She could only sit, still clutching her robe, replaying the scene in her mind. But somehow it wasn't the same: one time the bird flew through the glass without breaking it; another time, the window burst like a soap bubble and disappeared, leaving nothing but a sheen on the bird's feathers as he flew into the sun; and once the bird reversed direction and landed on her finger. She could see it every way but the way it had actually happened.

It was getting very hot in the room, with the radiator turned on high and the window closed. She reached a hesitant finger to the bird. There was a drop of blood congealing at the base of the slightly open beak; she wiped it with a corner of her robe. The feathers were glossy, shimmering in purple and green.

"Shall we go to Madeira?" she whispered, fanning the bird's wings between her fingertips. It seemed to her that they should.

She opened the window and arranged the bird before her and sat and waited...waited to go to Madeira.

Laurel Winter has sold a mystery to *Woman's World*. Of all genres, science fiction and fantasy intrigue her the most. She moved to Rochester, Minnesota, with her husband in 1982, having grown up in the mountains of Montana. It was there that she developed a love of reading and writing. She was associate editor of Jabberwocky, Montana State University's creative arts magazine, and has revised manuscripts for a literary agency. Now, Pegasus Prose, this book, and her twin sons keep her busy.

Patricia Hampl

from
A ROMANTIC EDUCATION

My grandmother, when she first came to St. Paul, got a job on the hill. To work "on the hill" was St. Paul lingo, meaning you were a maid or some kind of domestic help in one of the mansions along Summit Avenue or in the Crocus Hill area nearby. The hill was not just a geographical area; it was a designation of caste. It was also really a hill because St. Paul, like all romantic cities, draws its quality of personality, of identity, from its geography. Its topography mirrors its economy, its history, its image of itself.

There is a feeling of inevitability about the terraced, hierarchical topography of the place, as if St. Paul was bound to be a Catholic city, an "old city" as Minneapolis is not, as if F. Scott Fitzgerald, born here, was predestined by this working replica of capitalism — the wealthy above, the poor below — to be obsessed by the rich.

I always took Fitzgerald's side in the exchange he and Hemingway are supposed to have had about wealth. He was the hometown boy. But beyond my loyalty, I felt his romantic cry that "the rich are different from you and me" — a pure St. Paul cry — was more to the point than the answer Hemingway gave himself. *Of course* "the rich have money" — but it doesn't end there. Romantics are rarely given credit for anything beyond the flourish, brilliant, like spread plumage, of their style. But how often behind the indefensible rhapsody of a romantic statement — Fitzgerald's "The rich are different from you and me" — there is the hard fact of how people actually feel.

The rich get to live differently. They are therefore different. Fitzgerald's line is less chumpy than Hemingway has made us think. It speaks the case for many people and explains in part why there is such a thing as a celebrity in our culture. His unguarded cry is true, even if he was "romantic about the rich," as people say. His statement speaks more truly than Hemingway who merely got the last word in a conversation. Fitzgerald wrote the book on the subject and made it stick: *The Great Gatsby* is romantic and it says the harsh truth: that the rich are different because we — the rest of us and they themselves — cannot help making them so.

In St. Paul, the metaphoric significance of the hill was further emphasized by the fact that the grandest of the mansions on Summit Avenue, the one with a view only rivaled by the cathedral across the street, had been built by the city's chief resident, whose name was Hill: James J. Hill, the Empire Builder. Which is exactly how he was invoked in my family: the name, followed by the title. He had connected east and west with his railroad, the Great Northern; he had made St. Paul a railroad town, shifting its first allegiance, as a river town, away from the Mississippi so that even today the city turns its back on the river, as if it weren't the Father of Waters but a wet inconvenience.

This disregard for feature and advantage — the back turned on beauty — strikes me as American, but even more so as Midwestern. It is compounded of the usual pioneer arrogance and also, strangely, of diffidence: the swagger of saying we don't need beauty is coupled with the pouty lack of confidence of a wallflower who thinks of nothing else but beauty, but charm, which she lacks.

And so I became a snob...again. This time as a Midwesterner: the provincial anguish. My grandmother, I feared, had immigrated to Nowheresville. My family would have thought this nonsense. They loved Minnesota, preferred "a small city" like St. Paul, and without my knowing it, caused me to love it eventually too. But I spent my moody girlhood aloof from my town, saving myself for the World. A Midwesterner to my toes.

My mother always sighed seriously, "God's country," when we crossed back from Wisconsin or the Dakotas after a trip. "Thank God," she said, "we have scenery." "This is paradise," my father told us every year as we went into the dark of the woods to fish at one of Minnesota's "10,000 lakes" and batted at mosquitoes. "Mosquitoes? What mosquitoes?" my father said, glaring at the child traitor who spoke against paradise. "Look around you," he cried, gesturing with a casting rod, "this is heaven." He fished and my mother read her two-inch thick historical novels.

We were not really the Midwest, my father explained; that would be Iowa, or Nebraska, Kansas — hopeless places. We were the Upper Midwest, as the weatherman said, elevating us above the dreary mean. My father pointed with derision at the cars with Iowa license plates, hauling boats on trailers behind them, as we passed them on Highway 200 going North. "Will you look at that," he said. "Those Iowa people have to lug that boat all the way up here." My brother and I looked at the dummies in the Iowa car as we passed. "They're crazy to get to the water, they'll even fish in the middle of the day," he said, as if the Iowa Bedouins were so water mad that a school of walleye could toy with them in the noon heat, while my father coolly appeared at dawn and twilight to make the easy Minnesota-savvy kill. He pointed out to us, over and over, the folly of the Iowans and their pathetic pursuit of standing water.

Our supremacy came from our weather, and the history of our weather: the glacier had given us these beautiful clear lakes, my father explained. The glacier receded and — Paradise, with lakes. And as if the single great historical event, the glacier, had been enshrined as a symbol, in my family we were not to speak against the winter. Our cold was our pride. We watched the *Today Show* weather report and a shiver — not of cold but entirely of civic pride — ran through us as, week after week, some aching Minnesota town came in with the lowest temperature in the country. We did not delight in the admittance of Alaska, our icy rival, into the Union. We said nothing against it, but it was understood that it didn't really count, it had an unfair advantage which caused us to ignore it. "Didn't Alaska belong to Russia?" my mother said. "I mean, isn't it strictly speaking part of Siberia?"

Much better to think of International Falls, the Minnesota border town known on the *Today Show* and elsewhere as "the Nation's Ice Box." We took pride in our wretched weather ("St. Paul-Minneapolis is the coldest metropolitan area *in the world,*" my mother read to us from the paper) the way a small nation does in its national art, as if the ice cube, our symbol, were the supreme artifact of civilization. And like a small nation, we hardly cared among ourselves that the myths and legends, the peculiar rites of the land, were unknown and undervalued elsewhere, as long as we could edify ourselves again and again with the stunning statistics that constituted our sense of ourselves: the weather, the god-awful winters, which were our civic, practically our cultural, identity. I didn't personally hate the winter; I hated that there didn't seem to be anything *but* the winter.

The cold was our pride, the snow was our beauty. It fell and fell, lacing day and night together in a milky haze, making everything quieter as it fell, so that winter seemed to partake of religion in a way no other season did, hushed, solemn. It was snowing and it was silent. Good-bye, good-bye, we are leaving you forever: this was the farewell we sent to the nation on the *Today Show* weather report. Or perhaps we were the ones being left behind, sealed up in our ice cube for winter as the rest of the world's cities had their more tasteful dabs of cold, and then went on to spring. "Even Moscow! Even Leningrad!" my mother read to us from the newspaper, "can't begin to touch us."

"If you stepped outside right now without any clothes on," my brother said one day when we had not been allowed to go skating because the temperature was 25° below zero, "you'd be dead in three minutes." He sounded happy, the Minnesota pride in the abysmal statistic — which, for all I knew, he had made up on the spot. We looked out the dining room window to the forbidden world. The brilliant, mean glare from the mounds of snow had no mercy on the eye and was a mockery of the meaning of sun. "You'd be *stiff*. Like frozen hamburger," he said. "Or a frozen plucked chicken," regarding me and finding a better simile. "And when you thawed out, you'd turn green." The pleasure of being horrified, standing there by the hot radiator with my ghoulish brother.

We shared the pride of isolation, the curious glamour of hermits. More than any other thing I can name, the winter made me want to write. The inwardness of the season (winter is *quiet*) and its austerity were abiding climatic analogues of the solitude I automatically associated with creativity. "Minneapolis — a great book town," I once overheard a book salesman say with relish. And what else was there to do in the winter? Stay inside and read. Or write. Stay inside and dream. Stay inside and look, safely, outside. The Muse might as well be invited — who else would venture out?

The withdrawn aloofness of what had been, recently, leafy and harmless, now had a lunar beauty that was so strange and minimal it had to be foreign. But it was ours, our measure of danger and therefore our bit of glamour and importance. Or perhaps the relation between the winter and writing, which I felt was a negative one: maybe I hated the season and wanted to cover up the whiteness; a blank page was the only winter I could transform. That's how little I understand winter, how it can bewitch its inhabitants (for it is more like a country than a season, a thing to which one belongs), so they cannot say and don't know whether they love the winter or hate it. And we always said "*the* winter," not simply "winter," as if for us the season had a presence that amounted to a permanent residence among us.

Copyright © 1981 by Patricia Hampl from the book *A Romantic Education,* published by Houghton Mifflin Co. Reprinted by permission of Rhoda Weyr Agency, Chapel Hill, NC.

Patricia Hampl spends fall, winter, and spring teaching writing at the University of Minnesota in Minneapolis, and in the summer she writes at a cabin on the North Shore. She has been a Bush Foundation Fellowship recipient. A story, "Look at a Teacup," appeared in *The Best American Short Stories 1977,* and her books include *Woman before an Aquarium,* 1978, *A Romantic Education,* 1981, and *Resort and Other Poems,* 1983. Her purpose as a writer, she says, is to "make something out of what my family thought was nothing."

Juanita Havill

HOPE

Outside:
Waves of snow swell across the highway
A mean wind-whistle batters the roof
Squirrels abandon the bird feeder
Ice claims liquid for its frozen realm.

Inside:
Corduroy squeaks as children move
from window to window
Sparks fly from electric fingertips
Layers of blankets spread across the bed
The furnace shudders.

Deeper:
A pale green coil winds invisible
under the snow
tight spiral of purple-headed crocus
ready to spring.

Juanita Havill has worked as a teacher and translator and has published two picture books for children, most recently, *Jamaica's Find* by Houghton Mifflin. Her poetry has been published by local and national small presses, in *Lucky Star, Winewood Women,* the *Whittier Globe,* and *Peace & Justice.* She grew up in southern Illinois, lived and worked in France for five years, and came to Minnesota in 1979 with her husband and two children.

James P. Lenfestey

TURNING AND RETURNING TO THE NORTH

Outside the window people are rushing by, bundled in long, fur-collared coats, deep-pile lined coats, Air Force parkas, fur hats, hoods, swollen down jackets, wool scarves wound tight around the blue hair of old women, long, double-wrapped Isadora Duncan knit scarves in all colors trailing behind flowing bodies, behind smoking breath hurrying toward home in the zero-degree grey dusk. Sitting at the table, I watch them, working the cold stiffness from my hands, waiting to cradle the hot coffee, waiting for the steam curling up into my face, nuzzling my cheeks, defrosting my brain.

The young waitress is from another world. Her softly-accented voice floats down the row of booths like a feather. We all notice it.

Three stout ladies, unwrapping thick coats from thick bodies, notice it. "You know, she's not from around here. I could tell it the minute she opened her mouth." "Yeah." "Yeah." Their affirmations had a sharp, nasal ring.

I asked her.

"North Carolina." She breathed it, the "north" without an "r."

What part?

"The mountains: Ashville."

Beautiful country.

"It's pretty. That's about all you can say for it."

Her soft speech is such an anomaly here in the North Country. Not the quietness; there are people here who speak quietly, who chew their words before sharing them, or who are demure, shy, or terrified. But our speech itself has a harshness to it, the a's pushed up by the back of the tongue pressed between molars. The Midwestern Nasal Twang, as native here as winter and woods, a buzzing edge of sawblades absent in the North Carolina speech as it evolved from sea breezes in the palmettos, with the thick morning fog of the Blue Ridge, with three centuries of hot sun and living with Negroes. Her voice is slow and warm, layered over with a thin film of easy fat.

"I like it, except for the weather." She has been here six weeks.

Why here? Why would she come here to this flat North Pole? I think of my blood pounding in right angle intersections along the plain of my Midwestern heart. I think of my blood molasses-thick against the cold. That's why I'm here. I was born here. I love this flat, rich land, these footprints of freshwater lakes, this playground of blizzards.

I have just returned to live after years and years in the jumbled, piled up East. I was lost there, where the roads wander like the foot trails and deer trails they once were, where the water is salt.

The East was settled too soon. Where are those comforting grid marks of a surveyor's dream that superimposed order and school districts on a wilderness? To grow up here is to always know where you are, all roads being equally true: due north and south or due east and west. The exceptions prove the rule.

I was lost there where the towns proclaim for their significance at their city limits only their NAME and DATE OF BIRTH. DEERFIELD, EST. 1769. It is history that is the reference there, though the town may have burgeoned or died, or it may still reckon its population in Frostian neighbors-per-square-mile, rendering meaningless the essential Midwestern question: "How big is it? I mean, what's the population?" That's what we have on the signs at our city limits: NAME and POPULATION, proclaiming our twin miracles of existence and growth. We're still new and close to our conquest of the land, and each new body is still an immigrant in triumph (though history and honest original peoples are finally being "discovered" and maybe even, tentatively, praised).

Many a Eastern stone fencerow is now tumbled and lost in the 100 years of second growth forest, but their slow, heavy presence is still felt there as sure as stone on grass. The Northwoods are also honeycombed with fallen fences, but these are of wire, of various styles and barbs, all of which rusts and is more quickly and efficiently put up, more easily forgotten. They were not built one stone at a time.

Our virgin timber is fallen to gangs of immigrant crosscutters, stripped out in hardly an historical moment. The second growth, up after the blueberries, crowded out poor and rich fools alike — one seeking a plow and scratch grubstake on stumped land, the other with visions of vast northern cattle ranges. The trees seeded in inexorably and climbed before any but the deer had time to notice.

There were no endless generations here scratching hellish lives out of the soil, rock by crushing rock. The land was either rich and it had them or it was poor and they left. The move to the bottomless, rich prairie was too close, too soon. Who would, who could plow sand, pick rocks when under the sunset there was, free for the stealing from the drum and buffalo, topsoil deep as man's height and rich as cream?

Oh yes, the rocks can be pulled. There are Northern Wisconsin and Minnesota fields with cairns in their middles yet, some as big as haystacks and still growing, surrounded by aimless, cud-chewing Holsteins and Gurnseys. Milk land, the dairy farmers, the masochists, 6 AM and 6 PM, or 5 and 5, three hundred and sixty-five days a year, no Christmas, no Blizzard, this bio-production rhythm more relentless and true than Zen meditation. There is no time off, though babies are born and old ones die. The northern dairy farm can survive on marginal cropland. But most of the North is clay and rock and sand and swamp, good for berries and trees and turkeys only. Where wolves and Frenchmen and Paul Bunyan howled, now prowl maverick pulpers, timber combines, hunters and cacophonies of revelling tourists seeking the silence of clusters of trees, the touch of crystal waters (though wolves are also being "discovered," their sharp eye as well as their quick tongue). The prairie is now entirely under the plow.

There is some irrigation here, and more is coming, though the sky gods generally offer up what is needed, except when they don't. This flat prairie-cum-woodlands, woodlands-cum-prairie is natural growing land, ripe for making a nation rich in corn and milk and paper and timber, and still ripe for a dustbowl. So we count as being here everybody who doesn't freeze to death, and we celebrate it.

I am one. Carolina girl, this place is the skin of my hands, the sieve of my blood, the map whose co-ordinates I can find when the map is lost, when the lights fail, when blind; this is my web. This cramped, twanged speech is in my mouth too, though I underwent intensive purification rites in the schools of the East.

When you leave these steaming tables, Carolina, you will be frozen stiff. Your thin coat will blow around you like a bedsheet. Your room in the boarding house will take you and your local boy in and he'll make love to you like a blanket, a windchill aborigine whose blood runs thick when the wind blows and whose beard is coated with frost like candy. Neither of you will understand.

This fantasy has less grandeur than your reality. But why are you here? On the lam, of course, getting away from the small town and tyrannical parents, driven by ageless adolescent despair and itch. Anywhere is a liberating breath for you, even if the cold crabs your lungs like a fist. Even here downtown under glass and steel towers, downtown among the intensive culture of Commerce at the junction of prairie river plainess and Northwoods lumberjack bombast. Even here in flatland, in iceberg heaven.

You're 18 and on the road. Good Luck.

I'm 30. I'm home. Yes. Yeah.

Copyright © 1978 James P. Lenfestey. Reprinted from *Minnesota Monthly*, January, 1978, with permission of the author.

James P. Lenfestey, now forty one, lives in Minneapolis, Minnesota, where he is the father of four children, three computers, an alternate energy project, and a community newspaper, the *Hill and Lake Press*. By day, he is a writer and marketing communications consultant. By night, he is the Urban Coyote, columnist for the *Hill and Lake Press*, famous over a thirty-block radius. He teaches at Metropolitan State University and has finished two books for children and three books of poetry, including one of love poems entitled *The Sex Poems* to get the reader's attention. He is currently writing a book of short stories based on the misadventures of Coyote, the trickster.

To Order Additional Copies
of
Blossoms & Blizzards

PEGASUS PROSE

6423 13TH Ave. NW
Rochester, MN 55901
(507) 288-0779 or 288-4388

(Comments Welcomed)